Other Books by Mary Lou Eastland

Genesis: A Tale Twice Told

God, Soul, Reincarnation, Karma
A Spiritual Journey

A Love Story
For Bird Lovers

Rite of Passage
(Not for Children)

Coats of Many Colors
A Collection of Prose and Poetry

SEARCHING FOR
NIRVANA

MARY L. EASTLAND

Wasteland Press
www.wastelandpress.net
Shelbyville, KY USA

Searching For Nirvana
by Mary L. Eastland

First Printing – May 2018
ISBN: 978-1-68111-236-7

Printed in the U.S.A.

0   1   2   3

SEARCHING FOR NIRVANA

Nirvana: A transcendent state in which there is no suffering, desire, or sense of self, and the subject is released from the effects of karma and the cycle of life, death, and rebirth. Thus says the Buddhist. Nirvana represents the final goal of Buddhism.

I am not a Buddhist, I am a Christian. It occurs to me that for Christians, the goal is also Nirvana, though we call it by a different name, Heaven. And to the best of my understanding, Nirvana is the goal of Judaism, Islam, and, I suppose, every religion throughout the world. To arrive at a state of perfection and permanent bliss, what better could there be?

To reach the state of Nirvana, one would logically assume that he or she must strive toward perfection, that is, to become as God-like as possible. So, the first step in attaining Nirvana is to believe in and emulate God.

To speak of God on a personal level we must give a name to God. Most recognizable are God, Yahweh, or Allah as utilized by the three major, modern, Abrahamic or monotheistic religions of the world. The use of the words He and Him (though the terms she and her could properly be used as well) is strictly for the ease of discussion.

Once we give a name to God we must define what constitutes godliness. Who or what is God? What are the attributes of God? Here, the road gets bumpy.

Different religions have different ideas about God; that is, each has a god that is unique unto itself. If a religion supports the existence of one god, then surely, its god is the one true God, so the god of other religions must be a false god, right? Many, perhaps most, believe that their god considers them special among all humankind, and for this reason, Nirvana or its equivalent is limited to themselves and like believers.

There is no record, no verification that proves that God exists. There is only evidence and clues and the human spirit that says so.

There is no proof that there is only one God. However, even if many gods do exist, logically, one rises above all the others with respect to power, knowledge, and presence. This would be the god to pin your hopes on for attaining Nirvana, or Heaven, or Paradise. Isn't this what every religion is doing; worshipping who or what it considers to be the one, true God? So, the question arises, "Which religion is worshipping the true God?"

Though we call Him by different names and diversify and customize our own ideology of what He is like and what He expects; what attaining Nirvana, Paradise, or Heaven entails; what rewards are in store, it is the same expectation of a utopian existence that we all pray for and strive toward. Today, it is a foregone conclusion among the majority, that there is a single (if at all) God, or Creator, or source of all that exists. It stands to reason that it must be the same God that we all pray to hoping that one day, He will accept us into His abiding place.

The decision that each human must make is whether he and his fellows alone are embraced by God, or Allah, or Yahweh. Or does God, or Allah, or Yahweh embrace every human being equally? Has God, by whatever name we know Him, prepared Nirvana, by whatever term we use, for a fortunate few or for every man? This is the most spiritually pertinent question a person faces and must answer to himself. "Is, or is not, my God the God of us all, regardless of our many differences; race, skin color, religion, character, lifestyle, deeds?" If your answer is "Yes," then you are on the right path. If your answer is "No," then your path is leading you astray and you need to change course. If your soul has not asked, then you have much work to do.

AUTHOR'S PREFACE

I want to acknowledge certain limitations on my part. As I have continuously noted in other of my writings, I am not a scholar and certainly not an expert on the Bible.

My examination of the Bible began years ago when I read that theologians know that Adam appeared on Earth a mere six thousand years ago. And yet, my church teaches that Adam was the father of mankind, in other words, the first man on Earth. Knowing that humankind has been on Earth for eons. I believe it is obvious that if this claim of six thousand years is accurate, then the claim regarding Adam being the first man cannot be. If Adam appeared six thousand years ago, then he was not the first man and therefore not the father of mankind. I was confused and troubled. I wondered who had made the six-thousand-year determination and how they came to that conclusion. I decided to try and find the answer for myself. The only place I knew to begin, was with the Bible. If there is a definitive answer, I thought, then surely, it must be found somewhere within the Bible.

My parents raised me in the Southern Baptist tradition. Protestant Christianity has designated the Bible as the *Holy Bible*, the Word of God. The only bible that I was familiar with at that time was the King James Version. I knew of no other. So I began to search in the KJV, starting with the first book, Genesis. Immediately, I noticed discrepancies between the first and second chapters of Genesis, both of which supposedly describe the creation of the earth and of man. The narratives of the creation of the earth, of life on Earth, and of humanity found in chapter one and again in chapter two are incompatible with one another.

In my search, in due time, I received a copy of the *New World Translation of the Holy Scriptures,* which is the bible used by Jehovah's Witnesses. These two versions of the Bible are basically the same. Words differ here and there, but I saw no differences of any consequence. Not, that is, until I began to notice that wherever the KJV had the words "Lord God," the NWT had the word "Jehovah." Jehovah? Not only was the term never used in any of the discussions among my fellow churchmen, but never had I heard a prayer uttered to Jehovah. I tried it. I couldn't do it. Nevertheless, as I was to discover, it was the NWT with its many subtle as well as not so subtle differences from the KJV that heightened my interest in getting to the truth of the Biblical story. And so began fifty years of study which continues to this day. There is no end to the search for truth.

Long story short, I did determine, using the Bible's own timeline that Adam did indeed come into being between six thousand one hundred and six thousand two hundred years ago. This timeline, using the Bible's own information and without suppositions or what ifs or maybes, is shown farther into this writing. This timeline, with references, does not depend on educated guesses or theories, just numbers and facts as they are presented in the Bible and which do not require scholarly interpretation.

As I continued my research I discovered that there are numerous interpretations among scholars and theologians: variances of Biblical names, places, events, locations, authorship, quotations, and the list goes on. Explanations of the Bible's origins and contents are numerous and varied, the conclusions of sincere scholars, all seekers of truth. And of course, the actuality and authenticity of the stories the Bible relates will always be questioned by some.

As I have said, I am not a scholar, but I have been and continue to be a sincere seeker of truth. What you will find in this writing is truth as I perceive it to be. I would never presume my interpretations of the Bible's narrative to be the definitive answers to questions that have engaged intellectuals for hundreds of years. However, regarding the timeline presented here, I have utilized information found in the Bible rather than depend on the theories and suppositions of scholars where the dates of Biblical events are concerned. I have every confidence that the timeline presented here is an accurate account in as much as my computation skills allow. I am not aware that this specific timeline has been recognized and presented before now. In this light, please consider the results of my years of diligent and sincere truth seeking.

BOOK ONE

PART ONE

A DIFFERENT REALITY

This writing is largely due to my concerns with the Judeo/Christian revered book, the Bible. Within Christianity, the Bible has become an icon, designated as being holy, the Word of God. Although, it is not the book itself that concerns me. I am concerned with the way it has been and is being interpreted. As I know little of the Catholic version and nothing about the Jewish version, it is the Protestant Christian version, specifically, the King James Version that I have primarily relied on. The KJV is the Bible that I was exposed to in my childhood and youth and the version that I love and continue to hold in high esteem today. I have combined my study of the KJV with narratives of other publications, particularly the *New World Translation of the Holy Scriptures*. I have engaged in the viewing of innumerable documentaries on the Bible, considered the insights of many differing authors, and done research utilizing many different genres. I have also constantly prayed that God is leading me in the right direction.

Before getting into specific concerns, I want to clarify my own personal concept of God. I think of God as an essence, a wisp of pure, rarified ether that embodies intelligence and capabilities unimaginable and unattainable by man; the capability of engendering the material aspects of reality and of bestowing life to lifelessness. God is the source of and the perpetuation of all that exists. I do believe that God is not an entity, yet I/we are compelled to speak of God as though God is an entity not unlike man in order to define and discuss God. It is extremely difficult for the human mind to conceive of anything that is not material, not provable. But to understand God, this is what we must do. Belief in the immeasurable is essential. This ability can be defined as having faith, faith that there is something beyond man's understanding responsible for and essential to all that exists yet is not itself provable. It is this *something* that those who believe in a *divine being* refer to as God.

What I cannot and will not accept is the man-like entity that Christianity puts forth: an entity with human features, feelings, concepts, and, yes, shortcomings, such as sorrow, regret, anger, and vengeance; an entity with a propensity for violence, revenge, retribution, punishment, etc.; an entity with an insatiable need to be worshipped and praised; an entity requiring offerings and sacrifices, even human. This *is* the god of the Old Testament of the Bible. This is *not* the God I revere. This is not the God in whose image man has come to exist.

I want to state at the outset that I do hold the Christian Bible to be historically authentic, spiritually inspired and inspirational, God-sanctioned, and protected by God. I believe that every event recorded in the Old Testament took place.

Beginning in the book of Genesis, the Old Testament of the Bible contains a specific and detailed timeline that gives us the exact year of Adam's creation when tied into our current calendar. By following its timeline, we can ascertain the year of various other Biblical events, such as the great flood, the exodus from Egypt, etc. Granted, it is not easy to find, but it is there. Dates shown in this writing have been calculated using the Bible's own numbers, not mine, and not dates based on assumptions or theories. If you, the reader, should find mathematical errors, then the error is mine, not the Bible's.

The only date used from an outside source is the year of the final overthrow of Jerusalem by the Babylonian king, King Nebuchadnezzar II, in the year 586 BC. This event and year are not only historical facts but there is verification of them in more than one location in the Bible itself. Starting at this date and using the Bible's given numbers, one can count backward right to the time of Adam's appearance.

In researching sources outside the Bible, I came across the following statement (bold type is mine): "The Abraham story cannot be definitely related to any specific time, and it is **widely agreed** that the patriarchal age, along with the exodus and the period of the judges, is a late literary construct that does not relate to any period in actual history. A **common theory** among **scholars** is . . ." I cannot overemphasize that I am not a scholar in any way, shape, or form, but in view of the existence of the Bible's clear timeline, I must stringently disagree with these so-called scholars. I believe the Bible to be an accurate history of a race of humankind and not a collection of myths or an epic tale of angels and demons as it is often represented and believed to be by some.

As in my other writings, I will remind the reader that my current beliefs are just that, my beliefs. I am not attempting to sway the reader in any way. But I am compelled to share my conclusions on the outside chance that someone, someone who is having difficulty accepting the Christian message, will read and see a pathway to God. It is not necessary that you believe as I do. What I do hope, however, is that each of us finds a pathway that will return our souls, both individually and collectively, to a permanent oneness with our Creator.

Things that I was taught by the church as a child but that were difficult for me to accept may very well be the stumbling blocks that are preventing others from experiencing a personal relationship with God. A personal, one-on-one relationship with God is not only possible but it is His intent. All that is necessary is that you release your mind from fear and allow your heart to experience this relationship. The soul within you is aware of this connection. It has been there all along and will never cease to be.

I will be discussing many aspects of the Bible's message, but I would like to point out the topics that are of main concern to me. These are subjects which the church, in my opinion, has grievously misinterpreted and misrepresented. They represent the core doctrines of the Protestant Christian church.

Number 1: Is the god of the Old Testament God our Creator? Number 2: Is the Bible the Word of God? Number 3: Was Jesus God come to earth? Number 4: Is there just one path to eternal life? My answer to all these questions is an emphatic, "NO." These statements in the affirmative, are fixed doctrines within the Protestant Christian church. I am a Christian. But because I question these and other doctrines of the Christian church, I must specify that I may be what has been defined as a Gnostic Christian though not in the old traditional sense. Today's Gnostic Christian is one who recognizes truth according to his own soulful, intuitive intellect. A Gnostic Christian believes what his or her soul discerns to be true rather than blindly accepting prescribed, and usually required, tenets based on the time-worn interpretations of others.

In addition to discussing certain doctrines, I will point out some of the ludicrousness of thought where certain *miracles* are concerned. For example, Jonah's three-day imprisonment inside a whale. I believe that the majority of the Old Testament's so-called miracles are no more than natural events or are the manipulation of nature or some other contrived means initiated by a highly intelligent life form.

I believe that the Bible does not contain mythical tales, nor is it the Word of God; rather, it is a historical record of actual events. As I see it, all the stories therein, though some are apparently misunderstood, are not only possible but also are plausible, including the story of Jonah. It's the interpretations of these events that contain error. I understand the Old Testament of the Bible to be the historical record of the beginning of a unique race of man and its development over a course of several thousand years. It does not embrace the entirety of mankind. It is the record of a single race of man, the Jewish race. Aside from being a written history of the Jewish race, the Old Testament is also an inspired writing, having been penned by many different authors over a vast period, and in their own words, and who, most of whom, were all inspired by their belief in and devotion to their perceived God or to the religious sect to which they belonged.

I hope the reader will regard this writing to be, as considered by me, a logical, rational approach to interpreting events recorded in the *Holy Bible*. I believe that basically there are no crucial mistakes, though there are errors in both the Old Testament and the New Testament of the Bible. I do believe that various scribes and translators of the original scriptures have taken certain license over the years in presenting their own interpretations of almost all the Biblical events. I believe that many of these mistakes were intentional, written in such a way to influence the beliefs of its readers. Such is the way of organized religion.

Many misconceptions lie at the hands of the men who lived these events. However, they were victims of a very manipulative and, even by today's standards, an extremely intelligent entity. They worshipped a false god whose name, as he himself declared to Moses, was Jehovah. Who Jehovah was, or is, is an unknown. I will be sharing my theory on this subject.

But let us not cast a finger of blame on these early men. They lived as their lives dictated and reported events which they did not understand and were hard pressed to explain. For that reason, they touted certain happenings as being miracles. They reported these *miracles* to the best of their linguistic ability and in accordance with their knowledge of the world, which we now know was very limited. Neither should we cast blame on later scribes. All were performing, if not to the best of their understanding, then by order of the sects they represented. But now, lest blame be rightly cast on current church officials and theologians, we must cast aside all fear and reinterpret these *miraculous* events, using our God-given sense of rationale together with our advanced knowledge and understanding of our world.

To question is not to doubt. To question and analyze unlikely scenarios is one of the basic, God-given skills of the human brain. I do believe in miracles. I have experienced miracles in my own life. By miracle, I mean the intervention of some force that would have otherwise not been present. By miracle, I mean intervention by God or by His representatives. Yes, miracles do happen. However, anomalies of nature also happen, yet it is still nature at work. It is within the power of the human intellect to discern which human events are due to the forces of nature or the manipulation of nature, and which are interventions by other-worldly entities or forces producing what is, by our understanding of our material world, undeniable miracles.

Suppose that a man, a salesman, through no fault of his own, is unexpectedly let go from a job that he held for twenty years. It was a financial necessity on the part of the company. Over the next several weeks, he is unsuccessful in finding another job or any means of support for his family, but he doesn't give in to despair. In addition to daily prayers for God's help, he keeps a positive attitude. One day, he receives a call from his former employer. A job opening has occurred and they want him to fill it. Not only will he work closer to home but will be able to spend more time with his family. In addition, he will be making more money. "A miracle!" you say. No! It was not a miracle. It was simply God doing His thing. God continuously influences our lives, all our lives, without our knowing it. And He operates on a world-wide scale so that no one is overlooked.

Recently, there was a story in the news about a young woman driving home from work in one of the severely flooded states. She attempted to drive through water that was covering the road and was swept away by the current into deeper water. Her vehicle began to sink. The windows of the vehicle were all tightly shut, forming an air pocket temporarily keeping her afloat and alive. Several men swam out and attempted to break the windows without success. The vehicle continued to sink until it became completely submerged. Then another man arrived and dove under the water. He could not see her but was able to reach in and take the young woman's arm. He pulled her out of the vehicle and to the surface. She was alive. When the SUV was pulled from the water, all the windows were closed. And by the way, the hero was nowhere to be seen. How was the *man* able to reach through the closed window? How was he able to pull the young woman out through the closed window? Now you can say it, "It was a miracle!" God's angel appeared and saved the young woman. There is no other explanation.

Miracles occur on a regular basis all over the world. But even more powerful than spontaneous miracles is the continuous and continuing spirit of God at work in the lives of men, all men. Our responsibility, and our salvation, is to trust His will, His plan. Life is so much easier when we can release control of our lives to God, that is, to trust that He is in charge and is doing what is needed for our betterment and ultimate destiny.

I have spent most of my life struggling to make it the best life possible regarding my own and my family's health, wealth, and happiness. Forty years ago, my eldest son became ill. Our pediatrician quickly recognized the problem. "Get your son to the hospital. He has spinal meningitis." As I laid his feverish body onto the back seat of my automobile, I was shaking with fear. I stopped for a moment to ask God for mercy. Instead, I asked for something else. I prayed, "God, help me to accept your will." A great calm and sense of peace swept through my mind and body. As it turned out, it was not the dangerous type of meningitis, and my son recovered quickly and fully. After the ordeal was over, I thought back to my prayer request and realized that I had uttered a sincere, spiritually powerful supplication. It was a prayer based strictly on my faith in knowing that God wants and will bring about what is best for us.

Years later, after twenty-one years of marriage, I was divorced. It was not like it was after graduating college when I was fearless, had the world at my feet. This time, it was different. This time, I had two of my three teenagers in addition to myself to support. Having been a homemaker for most of my married life, I had no established career. I had been licensed to teach, and did teach for five years, but that license had expired. It would have to be renewed which in itself would take time and money that I did not have. But the biggest and most unexpected blow was I had no credit. The conundrum is that you cannot get credit unless you have credit. From my share of our community property, I was able to make a down payment on a home. But then came the expenses that I was not accustomed to paying: mortgage, home, and auto, and health insurance, utilities, car payments, food, clothing, etc. I was so frightened, stressed, and overwhelmed. Just to stay afloat was a continuous struggle.

One night after going to bed, I began weeping hot tears, desperate tears. I remember saying aloud, "God, I cannot do this on my own. Help me, please. I am turning my problems over to you." My problems did not disappear, but my fear did. My ability to cope grew with each passing day. And God and I have stuck with that plan to this day. That is, I leave God in charge and trust things will be just fine.

My recognition of the need to let God control my life was late in coming. But my spiritual awareness began when I was very young. Thanks to my upbringing, I was God-oriented from an early age. Yet there were things that I learned in my church that, even as a child, worried me. I thought that certain things I learned did not represent the God of love that I had grown to revere. I kept these concerns hidden in my heart throughout high school. But once I left home and entered college and young adulthood, I began to actively seek understanding. And my determination to seek and hopefully find truth with regard to God and organized religion came into full bloom in my early adulthood. My study, research, and prayer has taken me into a different reality.

THE AWAKENING, "ENOUGH!"

It's difficult to say exactly when my spiritual awakening began. I vividly recall what some would define as an epiphany, a flash of insight, a moment of sudden, intuitive understanding. I am going to say it occurred around the age of eleven. I can see myself in my mind, and I see a child, younger than teenage, smaller than twelve, so I am saying eleven. I was passing under the archway between our dining room and the living room when I stopped directly beneath it. I stopped to listen.

In reality, there was no sound, no voice, just the mental awareness of a message that seemed to flow into my mind from the cosmic realm, though I knew nothing of realms or the cosmos at that age. The message was: "You are special. God has put you here for a reason. You will contribute something of importance to humanity." The experience was so vivid that even today, sixty-seven years later, I relive the magnanimity of it every time I think about it.

It may have been in Psychology 101 where I learned that almost everyone has this same sense about themselves. We all want to believe that we are special among men. So, my epiphany may not have been an epiphany, simply a subconscious longing to be someone special. However, because I was in the act of simply walking through my home and was not in a contemplative or meditative state, because of the spontaneity of the experience, I tend to think of the experience as having been authentically spiritual. I have since come to understand that indeed each of us is special. Each of us is here for a specific reason with a specific contribution to make to the world and to our own souls. Whether we achieve that expectation, only God knows. I think not even the soul within us knows.

That experience did not represent my spiritual awakening. I recalled it for the purpose of emphasizing that at a very young age, I was God-oriented.

I grew up in a religion-oriented, actually, a God-centered household. My parents and grandparents were devoutly God-centered, and they instilled a devotion to our Creator in me and my siblings. With regard to religion, yes, we were also devoted to our particular denomination of religion, Southern Baptist. My father was especially devoted to the church to the extent that all family members were expected to be in attendance every Sunday for both the morning and evening activities. The only thing that kept us from attending church for Wednesday's prayer meeting was my father's job. His traveling kept him on the road and busy with frequent nighttime sales meetings.

Prior to each church service was an hour-long tutorial activity. The morning program was called Sunday School, and the evening activity was called Training Union. It was during these educational sessions that my mind began to wonder as to the validity of some of the teachings, beliefs, doctrines, etc. that my church taught us. Like those of most religions, we were concerned about what follows our physical death. We learned that there are two alternatives: Heaven or not Heaven, and the name given to not Heaven is Hell.

As I recall, I was around the age of thirteen when, in one of these educational classes, the *teacher* made the statement that no person who had lived and died before the time of Jesus would see Heaven. Why? As she explained, it is because they had not been saved by the blood of Jesus Christ. Jesus shed his blood so that we could attain Heaven. By his blood, we are washed free of our sins, and only by believing and accepting this would we see Heaven. I was horrified. It had to be a false belief because God would not cast trillions upon trillions of human beings into eternal torment, Hell, simply because they lived before the coming of Jesus. Of course, I dared not express my dismay openly, but inwardly I *knew* that this 'washed free of sin by the blood/destined for hell if you did not believe this' was a false doctrine. I believe in and admire and love Jesus and his sacrifice, but God is my salvation. It is God who forgives me when I needed forgiving. And it is due to God's unconditional forgiveness and love for me, no matter what the sin, that I will join him in Heaven when the time comes.

And then there is the horrific account of the flood. I can understand Jehovah's disappointment with *his* children; however, I don't understand his reaction. He decided to kill all life that *he* had created. Suppose our human parents acted in the same way, decided to get rid of their errant children. I know that some parents do. But loving parents don't. Loving parents forgive their children's mistakes, misbehavior, whatever. They give them another chance, try to rehabilitate them, give them a fresh start. Should we expect any less of God? But to destroy all life on Earth, even the birds and beasts, was un-godlike, ungodly. In my mind, if something is ungodly, it is not of God. I am sure of this. There had to be a better, truer explanation.

The story of the flood represents the very tip of the iceberg regarding the inconsistent, illogical, disturbing-to-me doctrines and various interpretations held by the established religion in which I grew up--the Protestant Christian sect of the Southern Baptist ideology. My concerns about what my church expected me to believe began at a young age. But it would be a number of years, during my college years, before my soul began to stir and say to me, "Enough!".

A CHALLENGING BEGINNING

Scientists have been able to identify certain eras, ages, or periods of time in their attempt to understand just how the earth and life on Earth came about. But man will never know. Man cannot know. Few if any human minds are capable of conceiving how the all came into being. I suspect that Albert Einstein or Stephen Hawking could be among the few. But I myself am perfectly happy with the explanation given in the first verses of the first chapter of the first book of the Bible, Genesis:

Genesis 1:1-5 ... "In the beginning God created the heaven and the earth. And the earth was without form, and void; and darkness was upon the face of the deep. And the Spirit of God moved upon the face of the waters. And God said, 'Let there be light,' and there was light. And God saw the light, that it was good: and God divided the light from the darkness. And God called the light Day, and the darkness he called Night. And the evening and the morning were the first day."

I have my own ideas of how the earth came into being, and the progression of life on earth, and the coming of the soul of man to earth. It satisfies both my spiritual and physical natures:'

Hydrogen, oxygen, methane, ammonia;
Lightning flashing throughout eons of time;

Amines, proteins mating, differentiating
And present all the while, the *breath* of life.

Simple plants and creatures now extinct;
Man of clay, man of mist
Up from the ground, down from the sky
Each quickened by the *breath*
But neither one knowing until,
Came the *soul* immortal

I quite easily accept the declaration in the first chapter of Genesis that God created the earth and all within it in six days. It is a beautifully written narrative of the formation of the earth, the beginning of life on Earth, and the creation of man. I do recognize, however, that it is a figurative accounting insofar as the timeframe is presented. There are numerous references in the Christian/Judeo bibles to the effect that with God, one day is as a thousand years, and a thousand years as a day. I would worry if I was expected to believe that God created the material Earth and its properties and contents in only six days. I think that some Christians do believe this. I think that the church allows them to think this, actually, even encourages them to do so.

Hard core Christians are staunch believers that the Bible, having been designated the *Holy Bible,* is the Word of God. Some accept it verbatim and adhere to the belief that it contains no errors or contradictions, though it is very apparent that errors and certain contradictions do exist. The foremost example of this lies in the very first book, Genesis, in the incompatibility that exists between the first two chapters and their common narrative. These two chapters describe the beginning of the earth and life on Earth. They are not in agreement with one another as to how it came about. In fact, they are totally incongruent. I was off to a challenging beginning.

Note: Throughout this writing you will find certain ideas, even words and phrases repeated. Forgive this ingrained habit of this retired teacher. If something is repeated often enough, it has a better chance of taking hold. There are certain findings of mine that I literally pray will take hold in the mind of anyone who is confused concerning the reality and nature of God, the truth about Jesus, the hope for Heaven, or the fear of Hell.

PART TWO

IN THE BEGINNING, GOD: ???? BC

The first chapter of Genesis is a beautifully poetic narrative of how God went about creating the earth and man. The time required was six days. After He completed the earth and its atmosphere, land masses, and distinct oceans, on the third day He caused self-reproducing plant life to grow. Then He cast the earth into orbit around the sun and gave it a companion orb, the moon. The sun and moon were for light during the day and night and to mark time and seasons. On the fifth day, aquatic life and fowls appeared. The beginning of day six brought land animals and various creatures of all kinds. And finally, toward the end of the sixth day, God said, "Let us make man in our image, after our likeness: and let them have dominion over the fish of the sea, and over the fowl of the air, and over the cattle, and over all the earth, and over every creeping thing that creepeth upon the earth." So, **God created man, both male and female in His own image.**

"And God saw everything that he had made, and, behold, *it was* very good. And the evening and the morning were the sixth day. Thus the heavens and the earth were finished, and all the host of them."

"And on the seventh day God ended his work which he had made; and he rested on the seventh day from all his work which he had made. And God blessed the seventh day, and sanctified it."

Though Moses receives credit for writing the first five books of the Old Testament of the Bible, it is generally accepted that he did not write the first chapter of Genesis. Credit for the authorship of the first chapter has been given to an unknown author or source often referred to as the Elohist. The word Eloah is a Hebrew term frequently used to denote God. The plural form of the word is Elohim, gods.

The length of each of the six days is unknown and is debated between and among scientists and theologians. It is not reasonable to believe that each of these creative days was a period of twenty-four hours. But it is reasonable to believe that each day was actually an era comprised of a vast number of years. The narrative ends on the beginning of the seventh day.

As each day represents a vast, almost inconceivable number of years, then logically, we must assume that the current era in which we are living *is* part and parcel of the seventh day of the history of the Earth. But there is no way of knowing. What we do know, as is evidenced, is that God has given mankind dominion or control over all living things natural to the earth.

It is apparent that a sizable portion of mankind lacks appreciation for all that God has created and given, as well as the responsibility that accompanies this inheritance. A large part of humanity cannot grasp that we, as well as everything in existence, have been formed by and are made up of the essence that has emanated from God, that *is* God. Every human being has sprung from the same source and houses within itself the same essence, or soul as we refer to it, which hopefully will one day return to its source, to God. There may be exceptions with regard to certain unreceptive, underdeveloped, unenlightened souls. Possibly, some souls are diminished to the point of being beyond redemption. Only God knows. Only God knows the final dispensation of those souls that refuse to accept the reality of His very existence and the role He has played and continues to play in our being. And only God knows if or when life on earth will end. Will there be an eighth day for earth and for mankind?

So, the first chapter of the book of Genesis, as recorded by The Elohist, is the initial narrative describing the formation of the earth and life on Earth and the beginning of man. Chapter two of the book of Genesis, as told by Moses, has it own narrative which is wholly incompatible, literally contradictory to the first. As one published, recognized Bible scholar, Halley, put it in his book, "Chapter two gives some detail omitted from chapter one; is not contradictory." But it is *clearly* contradictory.

JEHOVAH MAKES A MAN: 4156 BC

The beginning of the 2255 years of the patriarchs

Contrary to the first chapter, the second chapter of Genesis relates, first, the making of a man and then, only then, the making of animals, fish, and birds. As an afterthought, and for the benefit of the man having a companion and mate, a woman was formed. It seems that whoever wrote, rewrote, or translated this narrative of the beginning of life on Earth was unwilling to accept the pecking order in which life came into being and devised their own arrangement. Regarding the man, we are not told in whose image he was made. We assume that he looked like us. Regarding the woman, she was generated from a rib taken from the man. This action was neither a miracle nor a project involving sculpting as had been the making of Adam. Today, it is known as cloning. Let's take a closer look at this part of the narrative.

We are told in the second chapter that "...the Lord God made the earth and the heavens and every plant of the field before it was in the earth..." The Lord God? Not God? The Lord God! In biblical times, men often referred to other men as lord. Why did the ancient scribes insert this qualifying and even a bit diminishing term to the term God? It is a general term akin to the designation sir, rendering the expression Sir God. It was not until more than two thousand six hundred years after the events related here that the Lord God divulged his name. As revealed to Moses in Exodus 6:3, the Lord God's name was/is Jehovah.

The KJV of the Bible makes scant use of the term Jehovah. It is argued that Jewish scribes never intended for the Hebrew term JHWH to be translated into the name Jehovah. And though the accuracy of the use of the term Jehovah is debated, it is used abundantly and matter-of-factly in other versions of the Bible as being a more literal and appropriate translation of the word Yahweh or of the Latin term YHWH found in earlier scriptures. Regardless, the term Jehovah as an accurate translation of the term JHWH is not really the point. The point is that the entity represented as God in the Old Testament of the Bible had/has a name. And as learned in the book of Exodus, he wishes to be known as and to be called by that name to time indefinite. At any rate, chapter two begins with the Lord God or Jehovah making a man.

Just how did Jehovah go about forming his man? Jehovah "formed man of the dust of the ground." What does this mean? Surely, it does not mean, as Christianity teaches, that he took earth, or soil, added water to make mud or clay, and sculpted the shape of a human and breathed into its nostrils, and the clay structure came alive. I believe it means that Jehovah could utilize the materials of the earth to form a human being, a scientifically generated, test tube equivalent organism.

Seventy-five percent of the human body is water, hydrogen, and oxygen. Add salts, minerals, and nitrogenous compounds called proteins, arrange them according to a specific formula, and you are very close to having a whole human being. Breathing life into an otherwise lifeless organism is a given. Man frequently has to use this medical procedure, administering the breath of life. It is biological, medical reality, not a miracle.

Chapter two goes on to tell us that Jehovah called the man he made Adam, and Adam named his mate Eve. The Christian church insists that Adam was the very first man on Earth. The Bible does not say this, though it is obliquely implied in verse five, "...and there was not a man to till the ground." But, the first man on Earth? What about the various other and older hominids for which there is physical proof, not only that they existed but the age in which they lived, eras that came and went long before Adam and Eve arrived. Mankind, *Homo sapiens,* was on Earth long before Adam appeared. Surely, that is understood. Religious scholars know this. Why does the church choose to propagate the myth that Adam was the first man, the father of mankind, and then shrug their shoulders and look the other way when asked to explain? "It's just one of the mysteries of life that man is not capable of understanding," they say. I don't buy it!

Chapter two continues with the account of Adam and Eve in their utopian garden in Eden but the affair ends on a tragic note. Adam's creator, his god, Jehovah, cast him and Eve out of the garden and, worse, sentenced them to death. Why? Because Adam took a bite of an apple--this is what Christianity teaches its children--which came from a tree of which he had been forbidden to eat the fruit. Even as a youth, this troubled me. I was too young to understand allegories, metaphors, figures of speech, etc., so I was forced to take this accounting literally. No one offered an alternate interpretation except to say that the forbidden fruit probably wasn't an apple but then made no suggestion as to what the fruit was. I would later come to learn that it is generally assumed that the forbidden fruit was, in fact, carnal knowledge. Adam and Eve had sexual intercourse. But to continue: I was also troubled by the idea that God would place such a temptation, the tree from which the apple came, not only in the garden, but in the center of the garden where Adam and Eve must have passed by it on a regular basis. Why would God do that? To me, it was an unloving, uncaring, un-godlike thing for God to do.

Chapter three begins by accusing a serpent of tempting Eve to taste the forbidden fruit. But the serpent did not plant the tree in the garden. So, who was the tempter? Eve, in turn, took the *apple* to Adam, and he also tasted it. We all know what happened next. They were expelled from the garden.

ADAM: 4164-3234 BC

There is a chart at the back of this writing showing the Bible references used for determining the birth and death of the patriarchs from Adam through Jacob. I used this information to calculate the dates and eras that form the timeline I am presenting.

Jehovah proceeded to plant a garden to house and to feed Adam, the man he had made. The garden was situated in Eden and has come to be called, the Garden of Eden. It is reasonable to believe that Eden was in the area where the Persian Gulf now exists, which, according to satellite images, at the time may have been a land mass rather than a body of water. (If true, could this support the story of the flood?) Jehovah saw that Adam needed a mate, so he formed land animals, but none was suitable as a mate for Adam. It was only then that Jehovah decided to make another human being. He did not gather up dust from the ground. Instead, he took a rib from Adam's side and generated another human, this time a female. And Adam called her Eve and said, "This is now bone of my bones, and flesh of my flesh: she shall be called Woman, because she was taken out of Man."

When we oldsters were young, this idea was but a fantasy; science fiction we called it. In today's world, it is scientific reality. It is called cloning. If you are not familiar with the science of cloning, you should read up on it. You can Google "Dolly/Sheep/Clone." It is argued that Dolly was not a true clone. Nonetheless, the things that scientists are now doing with genetic material is unbelievable on the one hand and very frightening on the other. As initially reported, Dolly was a sheep that became the first mammal cloned from a non-germ or non-reproductive cell. Google "List of organisms that have been cloned." You will be blown away to discover the dozens of ways scientists have learned to manipulate human and animal genes. And it may disturb you, as it does me, to realize that man is so busy playing God.

In the center of the garden that Jehovah provided for Adam and Eve, he planted two trees, the *tree of the knowledge of good and evil* and the *tree of life*. Jehovah admonished Adam not to eat the fruit of the *tree of the knowledge of good and evil*; to do so would mean death. At the prompting by a serpent, Eve tasted the *fruit* and gave it to Adam who also tasted it, and they were both cast out of Eden for their disobedience. But it was not simply the act of disobedience that concerned Jehovah. There are several interesting points to be noted regarding this occurrence:

(1) The serpent talks. And apparently, unlike the serpents we are familiar with, it moved in an upright position. So, it was not a serpent as we know it.

(2) The serpent told Eve that by eating the fruit of the *tree of the knowledge of good and evil,* she would not die but would become *as* gods, able to recognize and discern between good and evil. Note the use of the plural, **gods**.

(3) What did Jehovah say to his companions? He said, "...the man is become as one of *us,* to know good and evil..." One of **us,** denoting several **equal** or like beings!

(4) Why did Jehovah drive Adam and Eve from the garden? In his own words, "...and now, lest he put forth his hand, and take also of the *tree of life*, and eat, and live forever..." This statement infers that had they not eaten of the forbidden fruit, Adam and Eve would have lived forever. Jehovah no longer wanted this for them. Punishment for their disobedience was banishment from Eden and eventual death.

The fact that, as it is inferred, Adam and Eve were initially intended to live forever confirms my belief that Adam and Eve were not the same genetically as other men who were on Earth at that time. And there *were* other men on Earth at that time and had been for eons.

Having been engendered scientifically rather than within a human womb, Adam and Eve may not have received spiritual natures or souls as those who are born naturally. It is the intangible soul within each of us that renders man the image of God. Psychics tell us that our souls leave the spiritual realm and enter the material realm, our bodies, near or during the birth process. Could it be that this was the knowledge that Adam and Eve gained from the fruit of the tree; that they did not possess soul natures and thereby were not made in the image of God? Was this the nakedness that frightened them so?

Yes, according to Genesis, they became not embarrassed; they became **afraid**: and Adam said, "...I heard thy voice walking in the garden, and I was afraid because I was naked; and I hid myself." Adam was not afraid of Jehovah, nor was he afraid because he had disobeyed Jehovah. Adam was afraid because he was *naked*, a condition that he was not aware of until after he had partaken of the forbidden fruit. Does it make sense that Adam and Eve were not aware of their physical nakedness and differences prior to partaking of the forbidden fruit? No, it doesn't. Was it a spiritual nakedness then? Were they devoid of spiritual natures or souls? It's a very plausible explanation.

They did hide among the bushes, and they sewed leaves together to help hide themselves because they dreaded being confronted by Jehovah. There is not one word to the effect that they were embarrassed and covering their genitals because they became aware of their sexual differences. So much for the original sin as touted by the church. So much for all the greeting card jokes and theatrical renditions. But they *were* naked, literally, so Jehovah proceeded to make "coats of skins" to clothe them.

In addition to their unconventional births, so were their life spans. The Bible records that Adam and his early descendents lived for hundreds of years. The oldest was Methuselah, who lived to the age of 969 years. Adam, himself, lived to the age of 930 years. This information astounded me, yet no one else seemed to notice anything out of the ordinary, or care. When questioned about this unnatural longevity, the reply was something like, "God's time is not the same as man's time,"- a day for a year, a year for a day, remember! Using that explanation, Adam lived for two and a half years as we recon time today. But I believed then that the figures represent actual ages. I still do.

The long life spans signify that Adam and his immediate descendants were genetically unique among men. They must have been genetically engineered hybrids, the result of mixing human genes with alien genes of some form. It sounds like what some believe that extraterrestrials are up to in this day and time. Maybe it is going on, and maybe it has been going on for a very long time--a very, very long time.

Genesis does tell of hybrid races--giants called Anakim and Nephilim, the results of the mating of the gods (alien beings) with human women. Extremely large human skeletal remains have been found. If you put a very large man in a fetal position, you would be close to the size of the skull of certain skeletal remains that have been discovered. And this would be one of the smaller giants. Some skeletal remains show humans as tall as a three-, four-, or five-story building. Go to the internet. You will be shocked. In Numbers 13:33, Israelites, encountering these giants, described themselves as being the size of grasshoppers both in the eyes of the giants and in their own eyes.

To think that Adam and Eve were half human, half alien would explain their long life spans. Either long life or some way of preserving and restoring life is necessary for extended space travel. Don't think it isn't being explored even now. Read up on the science of cryonics. What in the past was known as science fiction has now become scientific fact. The unknown has become known, and man continues to discover more and more of life's mysteries.

Continuing with the little nuances that caught my attention as I delved into the second chapter of Genesis:

(5) Adam and Eve "...heard the voice of the Lord God walking in the garden..." This made me sit up and take notice. Strictly speaking, grammatically, this says that the Lord God's voice was walking in the garden. This brought to my mind two visualizations-- The use of a sound amplifying device or system and/or, Jehovah moving about the garden in a mobile device that made some sort of

sound. At any rate, his movement about the garden made a sound that alerted Adam and Eve of his approach. That, or he was walking around talking either to himself or to someone else. Come to think of it, to think of God walking around, talking, goes against both the beliefs that God is ethereal rather than material, and that God has never been on Earth. God is spirit; too rarified, too purified, too perfect to experience the material earth. More will be said on this subject. Meanwhile, another contradiction by the church--it just cannot be both ways.

(6) When Jehovah discovered their disobedience, the blaming began. Adam blamed Eve, Eve blamed the serpent. Jehovah's first act of punishment fell upon the serpent, "...thou are cursed above every beast of the field...upon thy belly thou shalt go, and dust shalt thou eat all the days of thy life." This leads us to believe that prior to this proclamation, the *serpent* moved about in an upright position. And it could speak or could communicate by mental telepathy since it spoke to Eve, tempting her to eat the forbidden fruit. What was the serpent? It seems to have been as much human-like as it was reptile.

(7) Jehovah's second punishment was meted out to Eve. "... in sorrow thou shalt bring forth children; and thy desire shalt be to thy husband, and he shall rule over thee." Well, ladies, it seems we brought it on ourselves. If only some of our men did not take this so literally. We must remember that the human soul is sexless, that is, knows no gender. All souls are equal. For that matter, so are all humans be they male or female.

(8) Adam's punishment was the most severe: "...cursed is the ground for thy sake; in sorrow shalt thou eat of it all the days of thy life; thorns also and thistles shall it bring forth to thee...in the sweat of thy face thou shalt eat bread, till thou return unto the ground; for out of it wast thou taken; for dust thou art and unto dust shalt thou return." So, not only was hardship put upon man but eventual death. Of course, the punishment of death also applied to Eve. And Jehovah drove them both out of the garden.

(9) Then, Jehovah placed cherubim on the east side of the garden to act as guardians to prevent Adam and Eve or anyone else from

entering Eden. Most people would say that these were angels. Our standard imaging of angels is that they are human forms with wings, kindly creatures. But this is not the Biblical description of cherubim. See Ezekiel 1:5-24 for the prophet's description of a cherubim.

Cherubim were described by Ezekiel as four-faced beings, having the faces of a man, a lion, an ox, and an eagle, each face facing one of the four directions--nothing like we humans have ever actually seen or can even imagine as being a reality if indeed we are thinking of a living thing. Let's make a leap of logic here and imagine that these cherubim were not living creatures or beings but were *animated* mechanical objects that could see in all four directions at the same time. I suggest that these faces, like the cherubim placed along the eastern perimeter of the garden, were simply cameras that operated continuously as our security cameras do today.

In addition to these guards, Jehovah placed a "flaming sword which turned every way." What my mind sees is a searchlight constantly turning or revolving to light up the surrounding area. How many times have we viewed this scenario in the movies in the POW camps of WW II and in our modern prisons?

(10) And finally, the big question: Why? Why was Jehovah determined to keep Adam and Eve out of the garden? "Behold, *the man has become as one of us*, to know good and evil: and now, *lest he put forth his hand, and take also of the tree of life, and eat, and live forever...*"

Everlasting life: Isn't that the goal of every religion? Isn't that God's intention for every soul? Our souls, my soul, your soul knows it is on a round trip that began in the mind of God, was bestowed with the gift of discernment, has been privileged to experience material life and many other realities, and will one day return to its source, God. Unless...unless it denies its own Godliness and thereby forfeits its own existence and descends into nothingness. This, I believe, is the Gehenna, the hell, the destination for wayward, dark, unenlightened souls that have given in to evil influences and are without repentance and, therefore, have relinquished the mercy of redemption.

Hell is a choice, not God's punishment. The Greeks coined the word hell from the Aramaic/Hebrew word Gehenna. In Hebrew, the term Ge'hinnom refers to the valley of Hinnom. This was a location outside the city of Jerusalem very much like our garbage dumps, only much worse. Not only were decaying bodies and rotting garbage deposited there, but it was also used by pagans as a killing field, especially of children for use in evil rituals of human sacrifice. It is easy to understand how we arrived at our modern idea of hell. Well, it's not my idea, but it seems to be the idea of most of the world's population. And what a sad thing this is. Religion has effectively come to use the threat of hellfire as a fear technique, a control device. To me, the idea of hell, of never-ending torment as a punishment, is ungodly. And if a thing is ungodly, it is not of God. To me, the doctrine of hellfire is a false doctrine.

Continuing with the story of Adam and Eve, they had sons and daughters. The first son, Cain, slew the second son, Abel. Cain was a tiller of the ground, and Abel was a tender of sheep. When they brought offerings to Jehovah, he praised Abel's sacrifice of a slaughtered animal, but he rejected Cain's offering of fruits and vegetables. Out of jealousy, Cain killed Abel.

One question that is frequently asked among Christians is "Who did Adam's sons marry? We know that the descendents of Adam increased in great numbers. So, who did the initial offspring marry? Because the church maintains that Adam was the father of civilization, the first human on Earth, this question poses a problem for theologians. Without apology or undue concern, some, many, suggest that Adam's sons married their sisters.

I am sure that this, incest as it is called, did go on, just as I am sure that it goes on today and not just in remote countries or primitive cultures. But it is known that incest leads to the degeneration of the human gene. If widely and continuously practiced, incest would render the entire species extinct. I believe that Jehovah would not allow this to happen. No, it appears that Jehovah oversaw the mating and reproductive practices of his subjects. Why would I think that Jehovah kept a careful eye on his offspring to control their reproduction? Because he was building a superior race of man.

Because Jehovah, possibly the very first geneticist on Earth, was building what he considered to be a superior race of humans, he maintained tight control of their mating and reproductive practices. He controlled not only their practices but especially their capabilities. It was an easy thing to do for a master eugenicist.

When Cain was born, Eve said, "I have gotten a man from the Lord." (Shades of a future virgin birth?) After Cain, she again bore his brother Abel. When Cain killed Abel, Eve had another son, Seth. And Eve said, "For God hath appointed me another seed instead of Abel, whom Cain slew. Regarding Seth, the Bible records that Adam "begat a son in his own likeness, after his image..." Does this set Seth apart from his two elder brothers as well as his father by declaring that unlike them, he was engendered by man? Whether intentional or not, and I believe that the writer intended it, this tells us that Seth was a natural born child, a child born of woman, seeded by man. Though Adam was the supposed father or sperm donor when Cain and Abel were conceived, Eve gave the credit to Jehovah. I have to wonder why.

Nevertheless, as time wore on and the population of Adamites grew, Jehovah maintained strict control over the reproductive capabilities of the women, deciding when they would conceive and by whom or by what process. This probability occurred to me retroactively as I continued to study the story of Adam's descendants. This will become clear as this writing continues.

When Cain killed his brother, Abel, Jehovah cast him out of the garden, banishing him to the lands east of Eden that the Bible refers to as the land of Nod. In Hebrew, the word nod means wanderer or fugitive, or, to wander. So, the land of Nod could be a figurative term; Cain was cast out into the wilderness to wander. On the other hand, Nod might be a reference to an actual established settlement of that time. For all practical purposes, the Biblical narrative all but writes Cain out of the patriarchal line-up. The recorded genealogy of Adam's descendants begins with Seth. But Cain has a history of his own. Vast numbers of descendants emanated from Cain and played an integral part in the history of Adam's descendants, the Israelites.

To my knowledge, other than having sons and daughters, no more details are given about the man and woman, Adam and Eve, other than we are told that Adam lived for eight hundred years after he begat Seth. "And all the years of Adam were nine hundred and thirty and he died." (Genesis 5:3-5) At this point, beginning with Seth, we are given a genealogical list of the primary men or patriarchs to follow Adam over the next two thousand, one hundred, and eight years. Adam was the beginning of the family of men who constituted Jehovah's chosen race. They were Hebrews who became known as Israelites, who, today, are familiarly known as Jews.

Before leaving this chapter of Jewish history, there is one last oddity I would like to mention. The sixth generation from Adam was the patriarch Enoch. We read that Enoch was a very godly man in that he was devoted to Jehovah. Genesis 5:23 tells us that "Enoch walked with God: and he *was* not; for God took him." Every other patriarch listed "died" but not Enoch, "For God took him." This suggests that Enoch did not experience a physical death but that Jehovah removed him from the earth prior to death. If we are to take this literally, and I do, then in my mind it is yet another hint of alien intervention; intervention by an entity that can utilize and even manipulate earth's natural laws.

I have pointed out the inconsistencies between the first two chapters of Genesis which theologians purport to describe the same event, the creation of the earth and of man. Chapter one describes the formation of the earth, its atmosphere, its companion celestial bodies, plant life, aquatic life, bird and animal life, and finally, human life both male and female and both made in the image of their Creator, that is, possessing the spiritual quality of the essence we refer to as God. What follows is *my interpretation* of the account as we read it in Genesis, chapter two:

An entity who assumed the identity of God Almighty, wishing to create the ultimate life form on Earth, being a master geneticist and eugenicist by Earth standards and by using existing humans as models and genetic donors, proceeded to form a human being. He accomplished this by extracting certain kinds of cells from existing humans and scientifically manipulating and cross breeding the extracted DNA with that of a being not of this earth, an alien, possibly his own.

Thus, a hybrid human, a test tube, laboratory-grown human being was produced or reproduced. The first successful (that we know of) artificially engendered human was a male who the ancients gave the name Adam. Genesis refers to Adam's benefactor as the Lord God, a rather modern rendition of the term Jehovah which is a debated interpretation of the Hebrew Yahweh or YHWH. At any rate, the entity had a specific name, Jehovah. We learn this from the entity himself in Exodus 6:2-3, one of the few places in the King James Version of the Bible where the name Jehovah is used.

By the same process, Jehovah formed various animals to provide companionship and a mate for the man. As none were suitable for mating purposes, the entity took a bone from the man and cloned another being, a female, to whom Adam gave the name Eve. From these two hybrid humans, Adam and Eve, a new and unique race of man, came into being. Adam *was* the first of a new breed or race of mankind and the first of a long line of patriarchs of a people who came to be known as Israelites, or by today's society, as Jews. It goes without saying that other races of men were present on Earth at the time of Adam and Eve's appearance.

Jehovah prepared a park-like setting in which he planned for the couple to live and thrive. It was a closely guarded designated area environmentally controlled and possibly enclosed. In its center was what I envision as a control room, a center of operations. In it were historical archives, records of past eras, civilizations, and events. There must have been some knowledge or at least theories of the creation as told in the first chapter of Genesis. It was all-inclusive, including the entity's own identification, origins, and history and his research and experimentations on humankind. Also contained within was information that much of modern man fervently seeks: the fountain of youth, the formula for the restoration of life or eternal life.

Genesis refers to these bodies of information as the *tree of the knowledge of good and evil* and the *tree of life*. Adam had been warned not to seek out these records, not to eat of the fruit. To do so would mean death. Eve was enticed by one of the alien entities that the Bible refers to as a serpent to partake of the forbidden fruit. She, in turn, encouraged Adam, and he, too, sought the knowledge denied to them. So, Adam and Eve discovered many coveted secrets that they were not supposed to know. They learned the truth of their own being, that they were soulless, not natural beings, and the knowledge frightened them. Along with the serpent, they were punished for their disobedience.

Adam and Eve were put out of Eden. Jehovah did this to prevent them from learning the secret of eternal life. This implies that originally, Adam and Eve were not to be subjected to physical death. This is further supported by the fact that Adam lived for nine hundred and thirty years. Adam's descendants continued to live for hundreds of years. These life spans gradually became out bred and shortened to the ages that man's life expectancy is today, around ninety to one hundred years, give or take.

To prevent Adam and Eve or anyone else from entering the garden and learning the secret of gaining eternal life, Jehovah placed cameras facing in all directions on the eastern side of Eden, his center of operations, and implemented a searchlight, the beam of which revolved continuously lighting up the surroundings in every direction.

With the first two sons, Cain and Abel, gone, the bloodline continued by way of the third son, Seth. According to Genesis, Seth was the next step in a long line of patriarchs. In fact, Genesis presents us with a thorough list of the patriarchs, giving us their name, age at the birth of their own son, and their age at their own death. This list takes us through the first two thousand, two hundred and fifty-five years from Adam through Adam's descendent, Jacob, whose name Jehovah changed from Jacob to Israel hence the term Israelites.

If you are unable to accept my interpretation of Adam's beginning, and you are not inclined to research the Bible yourself, you may simply accept the timeworn, traditional interpretation presented by Christian theologians:

Jehovah took a sizeable lump of clay from which he shaped a lifeless form. The image or look that the form took on is not revealed. Jehovah then breathed into the nostrils of the clay figure and it began to live. The form came to be designated as a human and received the name Adam. Subsequently, Jehovah formed various animals as companions for Adam. We are not told by what process he accomplished this. Since none were compatible for mating and reproductive purposes, Jehovah took a rib from Adam and made it into a woman to be Adam's mate. Adam named the woman Eve.

Jehovah planted a garden to house the pair and in the garden, there were two trees of which Adam and Eve were forbidden to eat the fruit or they would die. But a snake came along. It moved in an upright position and, more significantly, it could talk. The snake began to tempt Eve with the forbidden fruit, assuring her that if she ate the fruit, she and Adam would become gods. Eve did taste the forbidden fruit and took it to Adam who also ate it. I suppose that to enhance the story, Christian theologians have suggested that the fruit was an apple. They do teach their young children that it was an apple.

The eating of the apple caused Adam and Eve to realize that they were naked. They apparently had not noticed this before. They were embarrassed at the realization that their physical bodies were different. They hid among the bushes and sewed leaves together to cover themselves. Furthermore, once they became aware of their physical differences, they began to explore them. In other words, they engaged in sexual behavior culminating in sexual intercourse. And although in chapter one, God had told them to be fruitful and multiply, this, according to theology, was the Original Sin.

For their act of disobedience in partaking of the fruit and for engaging in sexual intercourse, and after placing curses on them, Jehovah cast them from the garden. He cast them out of Eden to prevent them from learning the secret to everlasting life. Jehovah then placed cherubim or little angels to guard the entrances to Eden and a flaming sword turning in all directions, presumably to light the garden and reveal anyone attempting to enter. This, then, is the theological interpretation of the beginning of life on Earth and of mankind.

Before closing this discussion of Adam and Eve, I want to mention what was intended, I'm sure, to be a bit of humor. But in my mind, it represents a very profound thought or question, a true enigma. Though there is no way to demonstrate or solve the riddle, it should be taken seriously and thoughtfully; The navel is the remnant of the connection between a pregnant woman and the developing organism in the uterus or womb of that woman. If Adam was formed from a lump of clay, did he have a belly button? If Eve was formed from one of Adam's ribs, did she have a belly button? Did Adam and Eve have belly buttons?

NOAH: 3108-2158 BC

The year of this writing is 2016-2018 CE (formerly AD, now CE, Common or Current Era) The events discussed in this writing began over six thousand years ago or in the approximate year 4164 BC. I say approximate because there is debate over the accuracy of our modern calendar. From Roman to Julian to Gregorian, our modern calendars are arbitrary constructs. The calendar in wide use today, the Christian Gregorian calendar, is a solar calendar based on astronomical events rather than the birth of Jesus as so many believe. However, the number of years between Biblical events can be accurately determined by researching the Bible itself. As I have stated, the Bible presents us with a distinct and precise historical timeline. Except for the year 586 BC, all numerical data used in the calculation of this timeline is from the Bible itself.

The Bible presents us with specific events and time periods which constitute a continuing history from the appearance of Adam to an actual, verifiable, historical event, specifically, the reign of King Nebuchadnezzar II and the fall of Jerusalem in 586 BC. Using this information, we can say confidently that Adam appeared 4,164 years before Christ was born, or 6,180+ years before our current time. Thus, circa 4164 BC becomes the start date of the Biblical narrative of Adam and the beginning of the Jewish race.

Fast forward a little over one thousand years, nine patriarchal generations from Adam's appearance to the year 3108 BC. A very well-known descendant of Adam was born. His name was Noah. I want to point out that Adam was alive when Noah's father , Lamech was born. Lamech was fifty-six years of age when Adam died. Technically, might not he have sat at the knee of Adam, absorbing all the details of the Eden experience and subsequent events? Information passed directly from one generation to the next, or the next, would enhance the likelihood of it having happened and having been recorded accurately.

Noah is known for building an ark and riding out an extended rain that produced a great flood. Noah lived to the age of 950 years, but at the time of the flood, Noah was 600 years of age (Genesis 9:28-29). The flood occurred in the year 2508 BC.

According to the Old Testament and Christian theology, it was by means of the great deluge that Jehovah destroyed all life on Earth. Let me repeat that. A little over forty-five hundred years ago, apart from eight human beings, one man and his family, and a few animals and fowl, Jehovah destroyed all animal life on Earth. This really offends my sense of logic. If the church would compromise and say that the flood destroyed *Noah's* world and the life forms therein, I would have no problem with that claim, but the entire world population of both man and beast? It's an emphatic "No" for me. Forty days of rain would not destroy the entire world, nor a continent, not even a sizeable country. No, it was certainly not a worldwide flood. And neither all of humanity nor earth's total animal population was destroyed.

When I was a child, I was heartbroken to learn that God had decided to destroy every living thing on Earth, even the innocent. There must have been some innocent ones; how could animals and birds be sinners? As a child, I was deeply saddened. Had I been an adult, I think I would have been traumatized.

I had taken trips with my family and had an inkling of just how large the world is. It was very difficult for me to believe that there could be enough water in the clouds to flood the entire world. I still don't believe it. As for forty days of nonstop rain, that's a lot of rain. However, I have read that from August 1993 through April 1994, in an eight- month period, an area in Oahu, Hawaii, experienced 247 consecutive days of rain. That's more than six times the number of days it rained on Noah, yet Oahu did not become submerged. However, Oahu's rain may not have been as continuously heavy as that of the Biblical account. But it's something to think about.

Many areas of the world consistently experience lengthier rainfalls than did Noah's world. Now there's the key, Noah's world. As I said, if theologians would consider backing down a bit and say that it was Noah's world and all life therein that was destroyed by a great flood, I would find that claim acceptable. However, the claim would still have to be corrected. It was not *God* who destroyed Noah's world. God does not destroy. It was Jehovah who destroyed Noah's world.

Jehovah had become disappointed in his humans because they had succumbed to acts of immoral, decadent behavior. Violence and pure evil ran rampant. That is why he decided to destroy all that *he* had made. Though I still don't know why the birds and animals had to go. But he decided to preserve one man and his family. Do you suppose that he had considered the drudgery of having to start all over again, of having to create a new Adam and Eve? Instead, Jehovah chose to spare the man Noah and his three sons, Shem, Ham, and Japheth, and all their wives. This would be a new beginning for the chosen ones. How were they saved?

Jehovah could have taken the entire company of Noah's family away from the area he planned to destroy. He could have resettled them, along with selected animals, somewhere safe. There was plenty of world left to be inhabited. Or he could have taken them, as he had taken Enoch in Adam's day, and returned them once the waters had receded. Instead he decided that they would have to help in their own rescue. I suspect that this was yet another of Jehovah's tests of the loyalty and obedience of his subjects. He instructed Noah to build a large floating structure called an ark and gave him specific instructions on how to do it.

Jehovah instructed Noah as to the ark's size and what woods and materials to use. We find these instructions in the sixth chapter of Genesis, verses fourteen through twenty-two. This aspect of the story is very interesting. Without going into detail, the size of the ark was to be three hundred by fifty cubits. The exact length of the Biblical cubit is not known, so the ark's size can be and is debated. But it is generally accepted that when finished, the ark approximated the size of a football field including the end zones, actually a little larger, and it was around three stories high.

Without a local lumber yard and hardware store nearby, building the ark was quite an undertaking for four men. I have read that it took them fifty years. I don't know the source of that information. It was a formidable undertaking, yet the Bible says that they did it. But why so large? It had to be that large to accommodate all that Jehovah intended that it should carry. In addition to Noah and his family, the ark was to house two pairs of every species of animal and fowl, a male and a female, for repopulation.

Today, worldwide, there are over 10,000 named species of birds. Ornithologists believe that there are thousands in existence that have yet to be discovered and classified. Worldwide, there are over 8,700,000 species of animals, and more being discovered each year. These are facts. Is it believable that two of every species of the earth's birds and animals accompanied Noah on his ark? Or, just as incredulous, that this enormous number of species has evolved or appeared since Noah's time which occurred, as has been stated, a mere forty-five hundred years ago?

If the building of the ark was a gargantuan task, so must have been the preparations for its journey. The ark had to have contained many cages in which to hold the animals and birds until all could be gathered and housed before and during the voyage. The gathering of the animals itself must have been extremely difficult and time consuming. They had to find the animals, capture them, and of course keep a precise record to assure that they had not overlooked any species.

In addition, they had to gather food and store it, since the animals and birds were no longer free to forage for themselves. I have wondered how they met this demand. Elephants are vegetarians and customarily eat several hundred pounds of food a day. That's a lot of hay. Additionally, they had to clean the cages everyday, perhaps more often than once a day. As well as the chore itself, the odor must have been overwhelmingly unpleasant.

Logically, there were no polar bears on the ark, no penguins, no llamas or emus, no alpacas, and no koala bears or kangaroos. And there were probably no elephants on the ark either. But consider this, there was more than just one pair of every beast and bird. There were *seven pairs* of every clean beast and fowl, *and* two pairs of every unclean beast. The additional animals were for food and for sacrifice. To accommodate this many animals and birds I am forced to envision Noah's world as having been very limited in population, both human and animal. And his world must have been relatively small in area, too.

What we must understand is that the great deluge described in the book of Genesis, if it did happen, and I believe that it did, had to have involved a relatively small area of the earth, Noah's world, as I have dubbed it. What we must also understand is that Jehovah's people represented a relatively small population of humankind. And Noah's world or area of residency included but a small faction of Adam's descendants. Remember Cain? His offspring must have numbered in the millions, even trillions or more by the time of the flood. It has been suggested that it was Cain's descendants that Jehovah wished to eliminate. The chosen lineage was a very limited group in number at that point. We must also recognize that the animals indigenous to Noah's world represented a very limited number of species. And more importantly, we must concede that all life on Earth was not destroyed by Noah's flood. There is no reason to believe, that I know of, that the entirety of animal life including man has ever been destroyed by any means. Of course, the most important fact to accept is that God did not bring about the flood. The flooding of Noah's world and the killing of all life within it was the doing of *Noah's* god, Jehovah. Oh, and by the way, the appearance of the rainbow following the flood was not a miracle. The rainbow is one of nature's most beautiful occurrences and is in no way a miraculous event. It is pure science.

Following the flood, Noah's descendants began to increase in number. They were nomads or wanderers because they had no homeland, no land of their own. Having no place to settle and call home, they were concerned that they would become scattered and lose their identity as a kindred group. They decided to build a city, and they started by constructing a tower. It was a tall tower from the top of which they could see the entire surrounding plains.

When Jehovah saw what they were doing, he became concerned that he was losing his control over them, that they were becoming too independent. We can only speculate how he accomplished his next action. Mass hypnotism comes to my mind. He caused them to begin speaking various languages which forced them to break into smaller groups which eventually went their separate ways. So their fears had come to fruition; they became a scattered nation. The place where this occurred was called Babel, thus the story of the Tower of Babel.

As did Adam, Noah had three named sons, one of which was cast out of the family. It was Noah's son, Ham. You can read what happened in Genesis 9:19-27. Ham became the father of Canaan, the beginning of the Canaanites, the bane of the Israelites. Against the advice of his constituents, Canaan settled in an area for which Jehovah had other plans and paid the price, Jehovah's wrath. Meanwhile, Noah's youngest son, Shem, found favor with Jehovah, and Shem's lineage produced the next notable patriarch, Abram.

ABRAM/ABRAHAM: 2216-2041 BC

As I studied the book of Genesis, I was impressed at how diligent Adam's descendents were at keeping and preserving records. If you have ever thought that the numbers given in the Bible were random or just made up, were not important, you need to think again. You may wonder, as do I, how, over such a long period of time and such a nomadic way of life, they were able to accurately relate and maintain the records of events that took place in their own very distant past. But apparently, they did so.

As well as being diligent archivists, for the most part and due to their long life spans, main participants were contemporaries. In addition to being written down, their stories were passed on by word of mouth by those who had experienced the events. The word of mouth process stretched over and skipped over generations.

It has already been mentioned that Adam was alive when Noah's father was born. And though there were ten generations between them, Noah and Abram were contemporaries. Noah was alive when Abram was born and did not die until Abram was fifty-eight years old. So, there was plenty of time for Abram to get the details of the flood straight from the man himself. Although we are looking at a period of almost two thousand years, we are looking at the equivalent of three generations from Adam to Lamech/Noah to Abraham. Most of us have accurate information regarding our grandparents and even our great grandparents.

Just as Adam is the father of humanity within Judaism and Christianity [Islam sees him as the father of the Arabic nations and recognizes that there were men on Earth before Adam], Abram/Abraham is recognized within Judaism, Christianity, and Islam as being the founder of monotheism, the belief in one god. The worship of many and various gods was the norm at that time, yet Abram remained loyal and obedient to his one god, Jehovah, though he did not know Jehovah by his name, simply as the lord God. That was the persona that Jehovah had chosen to represent himself as to his subjects.

Abram and his kinsmen were herdsmen continuously on the move, searching for open land areas that could support their herds of animals; cattle, goats, oxen, and fowl, and camels, etc. Jehovah approached Abram, saying that he should leave his kinsmen and go into a land that he, Jehovah, would show him. Abram gathered up all his household and possessions and, with his nephew Lot and all his household and possessions, did as Jehovah had bid him and went into the land of the Canaanites. Once they had arrived, Jehovah told Abram "Unto thy seed will I give this land." Jehovah was promising Abram a homeland that would pass on to Abram's progeny. Jehovah's proclamation must have been difficult for Abram to understand since he and his wife Sarai were both old, and they were childless. Also, the land was occupied

As stated, Abram moved about continuously. Not being familiar with the geography of that area in that day and time, or the histories of the various populations, I find it difficult to follow the constant battles that ensued between the various tribes of Canaanites and between the numerous cities of the plains. But this is of no consequence because only the events discussed in this writing have a bearing on the dates presented..

There was famine throughout the land, so Abram and Lot went into Egypt for relief. Abram's wife, Sarai was a beautiful woman, and Abram became afraid that the Egyptian men would kill him to have her. He went to Sarai, and together they agreed that they would represent Sarai as his sister. In fact, Sarai was Abram's half-sister. They had different mothers but the same father, Terah. (Genesis 20:12)

The Egyptian pharaoh was told of the beautiful visitor, and he took her in with the intention of making her one of his wives. In return, he was generous with Abram, gifting him with much livestock and male and female servants. But before the pharaoh could wed

Sarai, Jehovah began dealing severely with him. When Pharaoh discovered he had been fooled, he sent Abram away.

I never realized it before, but apparently this tactic worked so well for Abram that he continued to represent Sarai as his sister as he continued his migration. Eventually, Abram and Lot's combined possessions became too large to continue together, so they decided to separate. Abram went to the South. Lot chose to go to the East, settling on the outskirts of the city of Sodom.

Once Lot left, Jehovah told Abram to look all around him in every direction, telling him that he, Jehovah, would give all the land that Abram could see to him and his seed forever, and that Abram's descendents would become countless numbers. Being childless, Abram laughed since at the time, he was seventy-five years of age and his wife, Sarai, was sixty-five years old and past childbearing capability.

Sarai had proven to be barren. There was no seed, no heir. In addition to their advanced age being a hindrance to the prediction, the land that Jehovah promised to Abram was homeland to other races and nations of people who would fight to keep their land. They would have to be eliminated. There could be no mingling of the races in Jehovah's plan. Out of concern due to the lack of an heir, Sarai sent her Egyptian maidservant, Hagar, to Abram to provide him a son and heir. And Hagar did conceive.

Feeling superior because she was with child, Hagar began to disrespect Sarai, and in turn Sarai began to deal harshly with Hagar to the extent that Hagar fled into the desert. As she neared death, an angel of Jehovah appeared to her, saying that she should return to Abram and Sarai, for she would bear a son who would be called Ishmael, who would father princes and nations. However, Ishmael would be constantly at war with everyone outside his own nation. And it seems that Jehovah's prediction of constant warring between and among Arabic nations came true, lasting even until this day.

Abram was eighty-six years old when Hagar bore Ishmael. Thirteen more years went by with no child for Sarai. Even though he was ninety years of age and had no lawful heir, Abram continued to receive Jehovah's promise that he would become the father of many nations. When Abram expressed doubt and asked if Ishmael were to be his heir, Jehovah said to him "...he that shall come forth out of thine own bowels shall be thine heir." That answer was certainly confusing to me. Was Ishmael of Abraham or was he not of Abraham? One should wonder. Nevertheless, it was at that time that Jehovah changed Abram's name to Abraham because he was to become the father of nations. And Jehovah changed Sarai's name to Sarah as she would become the mother of nations.

Another near decade went by, and Jehovah again appeared and gave Abraham a very unusual directive. Abraham and all of the male subjects of his congregation were to be circumcised. Abraham was ninety-nine years old and Ishmael thirteen when they and all the males in Abraham's company were circumcised. It was a ritual that was to continue and does continue to this day, even within many gentile nations. I believe that this demand actually had positive motives: circumcision makes impregnation or conception more likely so the race would grow at a faster rate; circumcision is hygienically beneficial, a hedge against disease and infection for both males and females.

Abraham did sire a son by Sarah. But before going into that, I want to broach a subject that was of interest to me as I read the story of Abraham. That is, the very personal relationship that Abraham had with Jehovah. It was more personal than you or I could ever imagine. Jehovah didn't appear to Abraham in dreams or visions or under misty circumstances. Jehovah sat and talked to Abraham face to face. He broke bread with Abraham, and Abraham washed Jehovah's feet. We learn this in the account of the destruction of the city of Sodom.

THE DESTRUCTION OF SODOM

Chapters eighteen and nineteen of Genesis relate the account of the destruction of the cities of Sodom and Gomorrah. It is a very unusual account because it speaks of Jehovah appearing as a man unto Abraham.

One day as Abraham sat in the door of his tent, he saw three men approaching and ran to meet them. He recognized one of the men as Jehovah. He invited them into his tent for food, water, and rest. They accepted and partook of his offerings. The powers that be within Christendom turn a blind eye to the contradiction this event poses. When Moses asked to see God he was told that no man can see God and live. There are verses in numerous books of the Bible, both the Old Testament and the New Testament, that record this. Start with Exodus 33:18-23. God appearing in the flesh, being fed, being washed, conversing at length? This exchange between Abraham and Jehovah, in my opinion, is stand-alone proof that Jehovah was/is not God. The god of the Old Testament of the Bible is *not* God our Creator.

Two of the men left and turned toward the city of Sodom. Chapter eighteen refers to them as men. Chapter nineteen refers to them as angels. Both chapters refer to the third man as the Lord unless, that is, you are reading from the *New World Translation* in which case the third man was Jehovah. Christianity teaches that the third man was God.

At any rate, Jehovah tells Abraham that he has received reports that the cities of the plains had fallen into moral decay and he has come to see if that is true; if it is, he will destroy them. Do I alone think it is odd that God would need to be given reports about the conditions in these cities, and even more strange, that He would have to physically travel to them to see for Himself? Does no one else see the absurdity of this? God is omniscient. He is omnipresent. God sees all. Jehovah was/is *not* God.

I must call attention to Genesis 18:22. It is a very strong indication of how certain facts are misrepresented, how words are rearranged to present a more desired picture. The KJV reads, "And the men turned their faces from thence, and went toward Sodom: but Abraham stood yet before the Lord." The NWT reads, "At this point the men turned from there and got on their way to Sodom: but as for Jehovah, he was still standing before Abraham." The royals of the world would cringe at this--Jehovah standing before Abraham. The

KJV transcribers and maybe even earlier transcribers were apparently determined to correct this breach of protocol. What a difference wording and sentence structure makes.

Apparently, Jehovah did find that the reports of the decadence of Sodom and Gomorrah were true because he did destroy both cities. The Bible says that he rained brimstone and fire upon them. I used to think that maybe what destroyed Sodom and Gomorrah was a natural occurrence such as the impact of a meteor. But, no, the Bible says that brimstone and fire "from the Lord out of heaven" came down on Sodom and Gomorrah. In other words, it was by Jehovah's own device, not nature. This indicates to me the use of nuclear power or, even more subtle, directed energy.

One hundred years ago, it was inconceivable that one man could destroy a whole city in one fell swoop. But that was before 1945. That was before an atomic bomb destroyed Hiroshima, Japan. Now it is easy to understand how Jehovah could have instantaneously destroyed Sodom and Gomorrah.

Abraham's nephew, Lot, and his family were living in or near Sodom. But Jehovah spared them by sending the two angels to warn them of the coming destruction. They advised Lot to hurry into the mountains for safety and not to linger or even look back. Lot's wife did linger to look back and died instantly. The Bible says she was turned into a pillar of salt. I have seen a photograph of a stone shaped like a cloaked woman, supposedly Lot's wife, near where Sodom is believed to have been situated. But that is stone. The Bible says she was turned to salt.

Have you ever seen photographs of Hiroshima after the bomb hit? You can see piles of ash in the shape of human bodies. Many people instantaneously and completely became incinerated in their tracks, doing whatever they were doing at the time This pretty much explains Lot's wife becoming a pillar of salt. She must have instantaneously become a pillar of ash by the blast. Lot and his two daughters had reached the safety of the mountain. Stone is the best, or one of the best insulations there is against radiation.

* * *

Following the destruction of Sodom, things returned to life as usual for Abraham. As he continued his wanderings, his deception regarding his wife/sister once again was discovered by King Abimelech. Though Abimelech had innocently taken Sarah to wife, Jehovah dealt harshly with him. I am underlining the words relating to his punishment. I am doing so not only to stress a point but also with the hope that you might see it as I do. It harkens back to the assertion I made in the discussion of Adam and Eve: Jehovah was/is a master geneticist/eugenicist who had implicit control over the reproductive capability and practices of his subjects:

Genesis 20:18. For <u>The Lord had fast closed up all the wombs of the house of Abimelech,</u> because of Sarah Abraham's wife.

Genesis 20:17. So Abraham prayed unto God: and <u>God healed Abimelech, and his wife, and his maidservants; and they bare children.</u>

Although "Abraham and Sarah were old and well stricken in age; and it had ceased to be with Sarah after the manner of women, she did conceive. <u>Jehovah visited Sarah as he had said and Jehovah did unto Sarah as he had spoken.</u>" I'm shaking my head here. Could it be more obvious what has taken place, Dr. J, at it again? And a *son* was born *at the precise time* that Jehovah said that a son would be born. Abraham was one hundred years old when their son was born and Sarah was ninety years old. And they named their son Isaac as they had been instructed to do.

On the day that Isaac was weaned from his mother's breast, Abraham held a celebration. Isaac would have been between three and five years old, which was, as I understand, the age that most children were weaned. Abraham was eighty-six years old when Ishmael was born and one hundred years old when Isaac was born, so Ishmael would have been between the ages of seventeen and nineteen. Sarah noticed Ishmael teasing and mocking Isaac, and it angered her. She asked Abraham to send Hagar and her son Ishmael away.

Abraham did not want to do this, but Jehovah appeared and told him that he should, and for him not to be concerned because Jehovah would preserve and bless Ishmael and make of him a great nation, because he was Abraham's son. So Abraham provided Hagar with bread and water and sent her into the desert. I have mentioned that the saga of Abraham is a bit confusing time wise. His own beginning and ending, birth and death, are clear and precise. What happened in between seems a bit convoluted, and this event is a prime example of what I mean.

It is indicated that the celebration of Isaac's weaning was when Sarah noticed Ishmael picking on Isaac and asked Abraham to send Hagar and her son away. As previously mentioned, Isaac was around the age of four and Ishmael was around the age of eighteen. Once in the desert, Hagar's water supply soon ran out, and death was imminent for her and her son.

The verses that relate this occurrence describe Ishmael as "the child," and at one point, Hagar cast him under a shrub in the attempt to get him out of the heat. The visual is of a mother trying to save her infant or young child. I think that most readers picture Ishmael as a young child, but he was nearing manhood. He should have been trying to protect his mother. At any rate, Jehovah delivered them, and Ishmael lived to start a new genealogical line. Hagar found an Egyptian maiden to be Ishmael's wife, and they had twelve sons who became the princes or heads of twelve nations. Ishmael lived to the age of one hundred and thirty-seven years. Ishmael did become the father of a large Arabic nation and according to Islamic tradition was the forefather of Muhammad.

"Many days" passed, and Jehovah decided to test Abraham. Jehovah instructed him to make a three-day journey to a designated mountain and offer up his son, Isaac, his long-awaited and only son, as a sacrifice, a burnt offering. Without questioning, Abraham did as he was told. Once into the mountain, Abraham built an altar and prepared his son for the slaughter. He had raised a knife to kill his son when an angel appeared and told Abraham to stop because now Jehovah was assured of Abraham's loyalty. Most parents had rather die themselves than harm their own child. It is sickening to see the degree of loyalty Jehovah commanded, or demanded

An eminent Bible scholar, the same one who said that the second chapter of Genesis did not contradict the first, said this, "That it was the voice of God Abraham could not have doubted; for surely he would not have set out to perform a task so cruel and revolting without being certain that God had commanded it. The idea originated with God not with Abraham." So it was God's cruel and revolting idea?

Surely, I am not the only one who sees the error, the grievous error, of this way of thinking. I cannot endorse this way of thinking that the church not only condones but promotes. Cruel and revolting ideas and acts come from cruel, evil minds. I've said it all along: Jehovah is/was *not* God. Yes, in my mind, the Christian church and Judaism are promoting a man-like god, a false god.

Some years later, Sarah died at the age of one hundred and twenty-seven, and Abraham buried her in the alien land in which they were residing and which Jehovah had promised to Abraham for a possession. This was to ensure that it was her son, Isaac, who would inherit the Promised Land, not Ishmael, the son of the bondswoman, Hagar.

Before his death, Abraham sent his most trusted servant to the land of his kinsmen to find a wife for Isaac to ensure that he would not marry one of the Canaanites among whom they were living.

ISAAC: 2116-1936 BC

Isaac's story is a stroll in the park compared to his father Abraham's. His most notable contribution to the history of the Israelites was his son, Jacob. As mentioned earlier, Abraham sent his servant to his kinsmen to find a wife, a woman of their own family lineage for Isaac, who was forty years of age at the time. The servant returned with a Syrian-Aramean woman by the name of Rebekah.

Isaac loved Rebekah and was faithful to her regarding marital loyalty. After twenty years of marriage, they were still childless. Rebekah, it seems, was barren. Hmm! Isaac entreated Jehovah on her behalf, and she conceived (another hmm) and bore Isaac two sons, twins that they named Esau and Jacob. At their birth, Esau came first with Jacob after him, and holding onto Esau's heel. This was interpreted as meaning that the older would serve the younger.

As the twins aged, Esau proved to be of ruddy complexion and hairy. He was a hunter, an alpha male by today's definition. Jacob was just the opposite, smooth of skin soft spoken, and possibly somewhat effeminate. He was a tent dweller. I take that to mean that he was a herdsman like his father and grandfather. Isaac favored Esau because it meant meat for his table. But Rebekah favored Jacob. One day, Esau came home from the hunt, famished. Jacob was preparing a stew and Esau asked him for a portion. Jacob said that Esau could eat for the price of the eldest son's birthright. Esau accepted the bargain. He sold his right to the family wealth for a bowl of stew.

When Isaac was seventy-five years old, famine again struck the land as it had in Abraham's day. Jehovah directed Isaac to go into the territory of the Philistine King Abimelech. Just as Abraham had been, Isaac feared for his life because of the comeliness of Rebekah, so he passed her off as his sister. This of course was not true as in the case of Abraham and Sarah. Rebekah was Isaac's first cousin, however. And, as it had been with Sarah, King Abimelech desired Rebekah and wanted her for a wife.

Isaac was very successful at digging wells. He went about the territory not only digging new wells but restoring wells that his father had established but that had been filled in by enemy nations, specifically, the Philistines. He succeeded at well digging and at planting and herding. It seemed that Jehovah blessed everything that Isaac did, and Abimelech's people noticed this and felt jealous. But they held a fearful respect for Isaac's god, Jehovah, so they did nothing to harm Isaac.

One day, King Abimelech observed Isaac and Rebekah behaving as a married couple and realized he had been tricked again. Remembering the punishment he had suffered for the sake of Abraham's wife, Sarah, Abimelech sent Isaac back into the wilderness.

Esau and Jacob were now forty years old. Esau had taken two wives from among the Hittites, a branch of Canaanites, which grieved Isaac and Rebekah. Nonetheless, Esau was the elder and by birthright would inherit his father's wealth and the promise of a homeland given by Jehovah to Abraham. Isaac was nearing death and very nearly blind when he asked Esau to go into the field and bring back venison and prepare a savory meal for him, at which time he would pass on his blessing to Esau. Rebekah overheard the request and came up with a plan of her own.

Rebekah quickly prepared the desired meal, summoned Jacob, and told him to take it in to his father so that Isaac would pass his blessing to Jacob rather than Esau. But Jacob doubted that his father would fall for the ruse. Rebekah then took some of Esau's clothing for the feel and scent and gave them to Jacob. She also tied goat skins to his wrists and his chest to simulate Esau's hairiness.

As soon as Jacob entered his father's tent, his father became suspicious saying, "How is it that thou hast found it so quickly, my son?" Jacob replied, "Because the Lord, thy God brought it to me." Isaac asked to touch Jacob which he did and said, "The voice is the voice of Jacob but the hands are the hands of Esau."

So Isaac passed his blessing to Jacob. Shortly afterward, Esau came in with the meal he had prepared, and Isaac realized he had been tricked. Esau begged for some portion of the inheritance but

Isaac lamented there was nothing left to give. Isaac's prediction for Esau was dire, "Thy dwelling shall be the fatness of the earth, and from the dew of heaven from above; And by thy sword shalt thou live, and shalt serve thy brother; . . ." And Esau hated Jacob and sought to kill him.

Rebekah immediately made plans to send Jacob to her brother Laban to escape the wrath of Esau. Isaac also wished Jacob to go to Laban to find a wife from among their kinsmen. Like Abraham before him, Isaac did not want his son to marry a Canaanite. And I thought this was odd; the proverbial closing the barn door after the horses are out, because when Esau learned that Isaac planned to send Jacob to find a wife from among their kinsmen--remember, Esau had two wives from outside the bloodline--he went to his uncle, Ishmael, Isaac's half-brother from the bondswoman Hagar to obtain one of his daughters for a wife. Meanwhile, Jacob set out for the safety of his uncle's encampment.

Let's look back for a moment because there is a definite pattern here with regard to Jehovah's chosen ones; the continuous breaking off branches of the family tree, infighting among brothers, good son versus bad son, favored son versus outcast son:

(1) Adam: The elder son Cain killed the younger son Abel and was cast out of the family. Six generations of Cain are listed in the Bible. Some believe that they were the wayward ones killed in the flood. A younger son, Seth, was established as the next patriarch in Adam's family tree.

(2) Noah: His sons were Japheth, Shem, and Ham, in that order. The descendents of Shem would provide the lineage leading to the birth of Jesus. Ham dishonored his father, and Noah put a curse on Ham's son, Canaan. The sons of Canaan would serve the sons of the other two. The Canaanites would figure prominently in the lives of Abraham, Jacob, and the Israelite nation. It was through Ham's son Cush that the participants of the tower of Babel and the dispersing of their nations came about. Jehovah would eventually demand that the Israelites destroy all Canaanites.

(3) Abraham: Abraham cast out his eldest son, Ishmael, from the family in favor of his younger son, Isaac. Ishmael became the progenitor of various nations of rulers and warriors. Isaac would produce the son, Jacob, the younger of a pair of twins, who would represent the beginning of the nation of Israel.

(4) Isaac: Isaac's eldest son, Esau, was tricked out of his birthright which went to his younger twin brother, Jacob, who inherited the promise of a land of their own that Jehovah had made to Abraham. Esau represents the beginning of the race of Edomites. Esau was destined to live by the sword. Today, his descendants remain divided nations.

Jacob was renamed Israel and became the patriarch of Jehovah's nation known as the Israelites. Although our story has centered around a single strand of the Adamic tapestry, at this point, twenty-one-hundred years after Adam, the descendants of Adam must have numbered in the hundreds of thousands, probably millions. The various tribes or nations became scattered over a vast area of what is now Egypt and other parts of northeastern Africa as well as what today we know as the Middle East. The ignored offspring and the outcast sons sired many children who in turn sired many children, etc. These various offshoots of Adam's lineage became multitudes of people with many cultural and linguistic differences. Among these were great kings and warlords. And though they were not Jehovah's chosen ones, they attained a cultural sophistication that the chosen ones had been denied.

Jehovah had carefully engineered the expansion of his little nation and had held them back in cultural advancements in order to control them. He held them to a nomadic way of life. He oversaw every aspect of their lives. He kept them subservient to him. However, he saw to it that they gained certain riches and assets, such as precious metals and artifacts and large flocks of various animals. They were wealthy and successful in that respect. Jehovah also ensured that they were successful in battle, seen as a mighty force, and feared by those they encountered.

Note: From this point on, the developing timeline will be determined by eras or time periods rather than by following the patriarchs. Isaac's son, Jacob, had twelve sons and a daughter, each of whom played a role in the expansion of Jehovah's nation. The first period begins with Jacob and all his family and company entering Egypt when Jacob was one-hundred-thirty years old, so the Israelites entered Egypt in the year 1926 BC, (Genesis 47:28).

The number of the chosen ones at that time was seventy. (Genesis 46:26-28). Think about that. From the time of Adam to Jacob at one hundred and thirty years of age, over twenty-two hundred years, the number of Jehovah's favored ones was seventy. They had a long way to go to fulfill Jehovah's promise of becoming a vast nation. However, from their entry into Egypt to their exit four hundred and thirty years later, their number had grown to over an estimated two million. Jehovah's promise to Abraham of a vast nation had come to fruition.

JACOB: 2056-1909 BC

Jacob's birth date is determined by considering Genesis 25:26. Jacob was born when Isaac was sixty years of age (2056 BC). Jacob's total age, 147, is given in Genesis 47:28. Jacob entered Egypt at the age of one hundred and thirty years (1926 BC). He was in Egypt for seventeen years and he died there (1909 BC). Genesis 47:28.

Jacob has given us one of the well-known stories taught to Christian children, the story of Jacob's ladder. When Esau learned that his brother, Jacob, had stolen his birthright, he set out to kill Jacob. With his mother's help, Jacob fled the encampment and sought safety with his mother's brother, Laban, some distance away. On his way to his uncle's, Jacob stopped for the night, and after falling asleep, he had a dream. There is even a song that tells of his dream, "Jacob's Ladder." Jacob dreamed of a ladder that reached from the earth into heaven, and he saw angels ascending and descending the ladder. At the top of the ladder stood Jehovah who spoke to Jacob, promising to be with him always and repeating the same promise that he had made to Abraham, a homeland and many offspring.

We cannot relate the story of Jacob without recounting the very interesting manner of how and why he came to have four wives. Jacob's uncle had two daughters, Leah and Rachel. Upon arriving at his uncle's settlement, Jacob first saw Rachel, the younger daughter. Jacob fell in love immediately and asked for her hand in marriage. As he had no wealth or means of support, he agreed to work for Laban for seven years for Rachel. In those seven years, he began to amass large herds of animals. At the end of the seven years, there was a wedding. In the bridal tent when his wife was unveiled, he discovered that he had married Leah. Laban's explanation was that he could not marry off the younger before the elder daughter. So Jacob agreed to work another seven years for Rachel.

In those seven years, with a little breeding trickery on Jacob's part and help from Jehovah, Jacob became very wealthy regarding herds of animals and possessions. And at last he could marry the love of his life, Rachel. By then, Jacob was ready to return to his home and his own people. He feared facing his brother, Esau, but his fears were allayed. Esau welcomed him with opened arms. And this brings us to the importance of Jacob in Jehovah's plan for his chosen ones. Jacob would father twelve sons, who, or whose sons would constitute the heads of the twelve tribes of Israel, which serves largely as the basis of the Old Testament narrative.

Jacob's wife, Leah, gave him six sons and a daughter, Dinah, who would become a priestess. Sadly, Jacob's favorite wife, Rachel, was barren. I cannot resist a wink here. When Rachel saw that she would bear Jacob no children, she gave her handmaiden, Bilhah, to Jacob for a wife and to give him sons on Rachel's behalf. Bilhah gave Jacob two sons. When Leah saw this, she became jealous because she was no longer productive, so she gave her handmaiden, Zilpah, to Jacob, who gave him two more sons. In different passages, the Bible refers to the two handmaidens as both concubines and wives. At any rate, together they gave Jacob four sons. Jacob then had ten sons, but he desired sons by Rachel and prayed to Jehovah to make it happen. Jehovah did make it happen (another wink) and Rachel gave birth to two sons, Joseph and Benjamin. Sadly, Rachel died giving birth to Benjamin. Joseph's two sons, Manasseh and Ephraim, made up the last two territorial heads of the twelve tribes. The tribes eventually split into two kingdoms, the Northern Kingdom or the House of Israel and the Southern Kingdom or the House of Judah which included the tribe of Benjamin. Benjamin's lineage would produce the first Israeli king, King Saul of the House of Judah.

Of his twelve sons, Jacob had a favorite, Joseph, Rachel's first born. This is the son for whom Jacob made the well-known coat of many colors. His ten elder brothers were jealous of Joseph and plotted against him. When a caravan of merchants passed through their land headed for Egypt, the brothers sold Joseph to them, knowing that he would be taken and sold into slavery. They ripped his colorful cloak, soaked it in animal blood, and took it to their father, saying that a wild animal had killed Joseph and carried him off.

Joseph was sold into slavery to a prosperous Egyptian. His owner's wife found Joseph desirable and attempted to seduce him, but he spurned her advances. She accused Joseph of sexual misconduct and her husband had Joseph thrown into prison. Joseph was an interpreter of dreams which gained the attention of a prison guard. The pharaoh had been having disturbing dreams that none of his seers could interpret. He was told of Joseph's ability to interpret dreams and summoned him.

Joseph interpreted the pharaoh's dreams to mean that there would be seven years of plenty followed by seven years of famine. The pharaoh made Joseph the governor over Egypt, second only to himself, and put him in charge of the food supply of the entire land. Joseph wisely began to store up grain in preparation for the coming famine. Egypt did experience seven years of plenty. Then came the famine just as Joseph had predicted. With the famine came Jacob and his other eleven sons.

JACOB'S SONS AND DAUGHTER
(Genesis 49)

By Leah	Reuben
	Simeon
	Levi
	Judah
	Issachar
	Zebulan
	Dinah
By Bilhah	Dan
	Naphtali
By Zilpah	Gad
	Asher
By Rachel	Joseph
	Benjamin

Levi was not counted as a tribal head. The tribe of Levi served as the priesthood and conducted all religious matters. Dinah was a priestess. Joseph became the governor in Egypt and died there. In his place, Joseph's two sons, Ephraim and Manasseh served as tribal heads. (See Numbers 1: 1-10)

ISRAEL ENTERS EGYPT: 1926 BC

Period Number One Begins
The 430 years that the Israelites were in Egypt

The story of Jacob's life has been simplified here, while in fact, it was very extensive, full of drama. The Bible's treatment of Jacob's history is somewhat convoluted and difficult to follow. At one point, Jehovah appeared to Jacob and changed his name. Genesis 35:10, "...thy name shall not be called any more Jacob, but **Israel** shall be thy name:..."

When famine befell the land, Jacob/Israel turned to Egypt for relief as his father, Isaac, and his grandfather, Abraham, had done before him. He sent his sons into Egypt to buy grain. When they entered Egypt, Joseph, now the governor, immediately recognized them. He sent them to bring his father into Egypt to live.

Joseph saw to it that his family was well situated. He knew that Egyptians detested shepherds, so it was easy for him to convince the pharaoh to give them a parcel of land of their own on which to settle. They were given the territory of Goshen located in Northeastern Egypt where the Nile River empties into the Mediterranean Sea. It was fertile land and well-watered.

Pertinent to the history of the Israelites while in Egypt was the emergence of what became the twelve tribes of Israel, headed by ten of Jacob's sons (excluding Levi and Joseph) and Joseph's two sons, Manasseh and Ephraim. Levi's descendants became the body of priests overseeing religious matters, the clerical body. Joseph had died in Egypt at the age of one hundred and ten years, and he was entombed in Egypt. (Genesis 50:26)

During the occupation of the Israelites in Egypt, their population increased in number to between two and three million (this is a guesstimate) and growing. This alarmed the new pharaoh. He instructed the Hebrew midwives to kill every newborn male child.

To save her son, a Hebrew woman of the House of Levi came up with a plan which proved to be crucial to the survival of the Israelites as a nation. That child grew up to become perhaps one of Israel's greatest prophets. His name was Moses. Yes, the same Moses who wrote the first five books of the Old Testament of the Bible. Every Christian knows the story of Moses in the bulrushes.

MOSES: 1576-1456 BC

Though Moses's birth and death dates have no bearing on the timeline, they can be calculated as follows: We know that Israel entered Egypt in 1926 BC. The Israelites were in Egypt for 430 years, so the exodus occurred in 1496 BC. In 1496 BC, Moses was 80 years of age (Exodus 7:7), so 1496 plus 80 equals 1576 BC, the year of Moses's birth. At the time of his death, Moses was 120 years old (Deuteronomy 34:7). So, birth date, 1576 BC less 120 equals the year of Moses's death, 1456 BC.

When Egypt's king ordered all infant male Hebrews to be killed, one Hebrew mother devised a plan to save her son. She took a basket and waterproofed it with pitch, placed her son in it, and had her daughter, Miriam, take it to the river and hide it in the bulrushes near where the king's daughter was known to bathe. The king's daughter did spot the basket and had her maid retrieve it for her. At that point, Miriam (who became a priestess and was active during the exodus) approached the king's daughter, offering to find a nursing woman for the child. The nursing woman was, of course, his mother. And so, the child was saved. The king's daughter adopted the child and gave him his name, Moses, because as she said, "I drew him out of the water." This is how the Hebrew, Moses, came to be raised as Egyptian royalty.

Moses grew to manhood. The Israelites had become the slave force in Egypt and were severely treated. A question that has been bounced about that seems to have no answer is, "Since Moses was raised as royalty, when and how did he discover that he was a Hebrew?" Regardless of whether or not he knew, it grieved Moses to see how the Hebrews were being abused. One day, seeing an Egyptian taskmaster beat one of the Israelites, Moses struck the Egyptian, killing him. Apparently, someone saw him, and word got back to the pharaoh. To avoid punishment, Moses fled into the wilderness and found himself in the territory of Midian, the home of

Jethro, a Levite priest. Jethro had seven daughters and gave one, Zipporah, to Moses for a wife. Zipporah gave Moses a son, Gershom, as well as other children.

One day while attending Jethro's flocks, Moses noticed a bush that appeared to be on fire. He went to investigate. The bush was burning but not being destroyed. Jehovah spoke to Moses, apparently from the burning bush, revealing his plan to deliver the Israelites from the Egyptians and Moses's part in the mission. By the way, indigenous to the island of Crete, which figured in early Jewish history, particularly with the land of Canaan which the Israelites and other descendents of Adam inhabited, is a plant called Dittany or Dictamnus, or more familiarly, gas plant or burning bush. The leaves emit and become coated with a very volatile oil. The heat from the sun can ignite the oil, making it appear that the bush is burning, but it is only the oil that is aflame. When the oil is burned away, the bush remains unharmed. No miracle at work here, simply nature.

Regarding Jehovah's plan to free the Israelites from Egypt, Moses was not amenable to taking part in the affair. After all, he had not been raised worshipping a single god. He had no idea who this talking god was. He continued to ask for signs of proof that he was indeed speaking to a god. He asked to see this god but was told, "Thou canst not see my face: for there shall no man see me, and live." If you recall, this was discussed in the section on Abraham.

Moses then asked for a name or title that the Israelites would recognize. The voice replied, "I AM THAT I AM . . . say unto the children of Israel, the Lord God of your fathers . . . hath sent me unto you; this *is* my name forever, and this is my memorial unto all generations." Moses was not satisfied that the Israelites would believe he had spoken with their god, and he pressed the voice for a more definitive answer. The voice then replied, "I *am* the Lord: And I appeared unto Abraham, unto Isaac, and unto Jacob, by *the name* of God Almighty, but by my name JEHOVAH was I not known to them." Moses got his definitive answer, but would it help him to convince the Israelites since they had never heard the name Jehovah connected to the god they worshipped?

Moses was not an eloquent speaker and gave that as an excuse not to participate in the escape. However, Moses had a brother, Aaron, who, as Jehovah offered, would be the spokesman for the two when going before the Egyptian king.

At any rate, familiar to Christians is the story of the ordeal of Moses and Aaron in getting the pharaoh to allow the Israelites to go into the desert supposedly to conduct a religious feast. The actual motive was, of course, to escape Egypt. Each time they would go before the pharaoh with the request, Jehovah would harden the heart of the pharaoh, and he would not give his consent. This implies mind control. Jehovah's control applied not only to the Israelites but to anyone, it seems. And each time, Jehovah would inflict a different, rather horrendous plague upon Egypt. This continued until nine plagues had occurred, and each time Jehovah would cause the pharaoh not to relent. And this brings me, again, to question Jehovah's motive. Why did he continue to hinder the exodus of his people if he really wanted them out of Egypt? But Jehovah himself gave us the answer. It was to induce fear into his subjects as well as their enemies by demonstrating his power. Control was the name of the game. Fear was the device. Absolute obedience was the price.

The tenth plague did the trick. The angel of death passed over Egypt, and that night, every first-born Egyptian, including the pharaoh's son, died. Every first born of the beasts also died. No one died in Goshen. The pharaoh demanded that the Israelites get out of Egypt. And so began the odyssey of Moses--the Exodus--in 1496 BC.

Note: In my book *God, Soul, Reincarnation, Karma: A Spiritual Journey*, I offer my own explanation for each plague, how it could have been a natural occurrence, or the advanced knowledge of an imminent event, or the manipulation of nature responsible. But it was the final plague, the death of every Egyptian first born, that pretty much defies explanation, though I am sure that there is one. I have my own theory.

ISRAEL EXITS EGYPT:
1496 BC
Period Number One Ends
The Exodus

There are so many disagreements among Bible scholars regarding dates, names, events, etc. I have read that there are monumental differences of opinion as to the date of the exodus of the Israelites from Egypt. Some say it occurred in the thirteenth century BC and others in the fifteenth century BC. Some say it didn't happen at all because there is no mention of Israelites having occupied Egypt in Egyptian historical records. But the Bible tells us that not only did the Israelites dwell in the land of Goshen in Egypt, but that they were in Egypt for four hundred and thirty years. (see Exodus 12:40-41) The Bible's timeline informs us that the exodus occurred near the beginning of the fifteenth century BC, specifically, in 1496 BC.

There are very few people who do not know of the story of the Israelites' exodus from Egypt. People of religions other than Judaism know the basic story, but Christians especially are familiar with it. However, I believe that many Christians are not at all knowledgeable about the many revealing and, in most cases, horrendous details surrounding the ordeal, and it was an ordeal in every sense of the word. After being in Egypt for four hundred and thirty years, the Israelites began their departure.

To prevent bogging down with the scores of significant events that took place during their years of wandering in the wilderness, I am mentioning just those that piqued my interest. To begin with, there is the number of people involved. There were more than six hundred thousand (600,000) able-bodied men. (Exodus 12:37-38 and Numbers 1:45-47). That means males twenty years of age and older who could go into battle. Add to that both younger and older males, the children, and the infirm. Women were not included in head counts, so we must add to the total number, the grandmothers, mothers, wives, sisters, daughters, concubines, and servants. Also, the Levites were not included in this count. The figure rises to well over two million. And this may be a conservative figure as families consisted often of several wives and numerous children. But we will go with two million plus, an average of four for each able-bodied male.

Now consider the flocks of cattle, oxen, sheep, goats, fowl, and other animals, which certainly outnumbered the people, that had to be herded along. Also consider the possessions that had to be brought with them: tents, tools, household items, clothing, food, written materials, personal items, and of course their valuables--everything they owned. We know they had items made of gold as later they fashioned a calf of gold to worship. This was no camp meeting, it was quite an entourage. Try to visualize it. It is almost beyond comprehension. With such a massive gathering, the procedure had to have been strictly, follow the crowd.

Before their time in Egypt, the Israelites were a people of nomadic existence. They had been deprived of their homeland by Jehovah, first, when he drove Adam and Eve out of Eden, and again when Jehovah destroyed Noah's world with the flood, and yet again when Jehovah scattered the nation at the tower of Babel. But Jehovah had a plan for his people, and he would not allow his plan to be waylaid or altered.

When the Israelites left Egypt, they had no place to go. They were forced to wander about in what the Bible refers to as the land of their alien residences. This largely included the lands of Canaan with its numerous offshoot tribes of Adam's descendants represented today by the Arabic nations. It had been over six hundred years since Jehovah had made the promise to Abraham that he would make of him a great nation and would establish a homeland for them, a land flowing with milk and honey. The great, or at least sizeable, nation had come to be. At that point, one would assume that Jehovah was going to lead the Israelites to the "Promised Land."

The next thing that I thought odd was the direction in which they went. Numerous maps of their supposed route and possible routes can be found on the internet. Keep in mind that although Moses was the leader of the group, the one doing the leading was Jehovah. Moses didn't know where they were going, but Jehovah did. And it was not open land free for the taking. It was a territory occupied by people who were not sympathetic to the Israelites and who would fight to defend their territory.

Had Jehovah led them on a direct, easterly route, the migration might not have been the lengthy ordeal that it became. This would, however, have taken them over land that was occupied by the very dangerous Philistines, the land of the giants. As it turned out, they still had to fight their way, all the way, to the intended destination. And as we later learn, the forty years was not a necessary element; it was a punishment for their loss of faith in Jehovah and for their many disobediences to him along the way.

There are several proposed routes that Moses and the Israelites took. There is no definitive information, only supposition based on individual interpretations of the Biblical account. But to avoid the Philistines, Jehovah led the Israelites south to a dead end, to the shore of the now Gulf of Suez, an arm of the Red Sea. Here occurred the miraculous crossing of the entire crowd over that arm of the waters of the Red Sea to the safety of the opposite shore. By then, the Egyptians realized what was happening: their slave force was escaping, and they were in close pursuit of the Israelites to take them back to Egypt. Unfortunately for the pursuing Egyptians, as they attempted to make the crossing, the sea swallowed them up.

There have been numerous explanations offered for how the crossing of the Red Sea, the Gulf of Suez, was possible, including my own explanation in another writing. Suffice it to say that the *miraculous* crossing was accomplished due to Jehovah's advanced development and intelligence. His understanding of and command of Earth's natural laws enabled him to manipulate those laws, resulting in supernatural, or should I say supra-natural, events.

There is argument that the crossing occurred at an isthmus or natural land bridge that lies between the Mediterranean Sea on the north and the Gulf of Suez on the south But, that would have made Jehovah's intervention by parting the sea unnecessary. We're going to stick with the story and accept at face value that the parting of the sea did take place. The waters parted, forming a wall on both sides of the pathway.

So their god, Jehovah, led the escape. Just how did he go about this? Did he use mental telepathy to instruct Moses where to travel, ride before the Israelites on horseback, drive a chariot, walk alongside Moses and Aaron? If that sounds ludicrous, consider how Jehovah did lead them. He led them from a within a cloud.

Jehovah was concealed in a cloud that went before them by day. At night, it appeared as a pillar of fire to light the way. To me, this harkens back to the flaming sword (beam or pillar of light) that Jehovah left behind to guard the entrance to Eden. Together, in my mind, the cloud and the pillar of fire suggest something else, such as an airborne craft of some sort, one that was under intelligent control, was extremely maneuverable, and could hover without the need to land.

Upon crossing the Red Sea, the Israelites had as far to go to reach their destination, the "Promised Land," if not farther than they had already traveled. They did not travel in a direct path but one that wound serpentine up and down, round and round. Between where they were and where they wanted to be were many enemies, various tribes of Canaanites which would have to be conquered in battle. Jehovah did not intend to move the Israelites around these hostile groups. His intention was to confront them and destroy them. Upon nearing their destination, Jehovah instructed Moses to select one man from each of the twelve tribes to reconnoiter or spy out the territories through which they would have to pass. Among these twelve was Joshua, who would later eplace Moses.

They spied out the land for forty days. They observed giants, the Anakim or sons of Anak in some of the territories. Here was born the aforementioned phrase, "We were in our own sight as grasshoppers, and so we were in their sight." Upon returning to Moses, ten of the men were fearful and unwilling to confront the enemy. Only Joshua and Caleb were ready to go into battle with the enemy as Jehovah intended them to do. As a punishment for their lack of faith and obedience, Jehovah caused the entire congregation to wander the wilderness for forty years, a year for each day the men spied out the land. All the original six hundred thousand men of military age who had walked out of Egypt as able-bodied men, by some means or another, died. Apart from Joshua and Caleb, none of the fighting force entered the Promised Land. (See Numbers 14:29-34 and Joshua 5:6)

Shockingly, neither did Jehovah allow Moses or Aaron to enter the Promised Land. Aaron had died earlier. But Moses was living when they reached the Jordan River which they would have to cross to enter the Promise Land.

During the wilderness ordeal, Jehovah had commanded Moses to strike a rock, promising to make much needed water flow out of it. Moses obeyed and the people had water. Later, God told Moses to speak to a rock, to make water flow in the desert again. However, Moses struck the rock as before instead of speaking to it. Because of this one act of disobedience, or misunderstanding, God told Moses that he would not be permitted to bring the people into the Promised Land. And later, as decreed, as Moses looked across the Jordan River upon the Promised Land, toward the city of Jericho, Jehovah commanded Moses to die (?). And Moses died there (?). (See Deut 34:4-7) "And Moses was an hundred and twenty years old when he died: his eye was not dim, nor his natural force abated." I wonder *how* he died.

The entry into the long-awaited Promised Land began with another miraculous crossing of a body of water. As at the Red Sea, by parting the waters, Jehovah provided a dry pathway across the Jordan River. There was a notable difference, however. At the Red Sea, the water stood up, forming a wall on both sides of the crossing. At the Jordan River, a wall of water was formed on the high side while the water below the wall flowed away. I thought this was an interesting detail, and wondered, why the difference?

It occurred to me that Jehovah seems to have had a specific motive in all that he did, either to show his power to solicit fear, praise and obedience, or to destroy. What better way to destroy all the pursuing Egyptians in one fell swoop at the Red Sea than to have the water come crashing down upon them from all sides. There was no chance of anyone surviving. Total destruction, one of Jehovah's frequent actions as we have seen and will continue to see.

Before being able to inhabit the Promised Land, they had to fight one final battle. The city of Jericho was well established and occupied and had to be captured. With Moses and Aaron now gone, Joshua took over leadership of the Israelites and led the Israelites into the battle for the city of Jericho.

The battle for Jericho is an extremely interesting account in the Bible. I see it as a prime demonstration of how the manipulation of natural laws can be utilized to bring about a desired outcome; in this case, the collapse of the walls surrounding the city. You can read this account in the sixth chapter of the book of Joshua. Keep in mind these two conditions: cadence and vibration. I have been told that if a military unit is marching in cadence, when they come to a bridge they break step. If they did not, the vibrations of their marching cadence would collapse the bridge. And it seems this was the case with the walls of Jericho. The Israelites marched in step seven times around the city, shouted in unison, and the priests blew horns. The walls succumbed to the vibrations produced by sustained, intense movement and sound.

Upon taking control of the city, at Jehovah's command, except for one woman and her family who had concealed and protected the men who had spied out the land, the Israelites murdered every man, woman, child and beast and burned the city to the ground. This was by Jehovah's command. Take no prisoners. This was his pattern.

But I am getting ahead of myself because we are now forty years into the next period in the Bible's timeline. However, before moving on from the exodus and the subsequent forty-year ordeal in the wilderness, I feel compelled to mention what I consider a graphic example of the fact that Jehovah was/is not the loving, forgiving God that Christianity purports to worship.

Jehovah proclaimed himself to be "a vengeful god" and a "manly god of war." There are many, many examples throughout the Old Testament narrative which lend truth to his claims. But his vengeful, evil nature is clearly demonstrated by events described in the book of Numbers. It is no wonder that he was feared so, as some fear God today.

The Israelites were forbidden to do any work on the Sabbath day. What would happen if they did? When they discovered a man gathering sticks on the Sabbath, they went to Moses who went to Jehovah to determine his punishment. Jehovah decreed that he be stoned to death, and so he was. (See Numbers 15:32-36).

There was a distinct segregation between the priestly members from the tribe of Levi and the masses of Israelites. The masses had become tired of all the rules and regulations put upon them and the lording over them by Moses and Aaron and the priests. They felt that they had no voice because non-priestly members could not approach Jehovah. Those who dared to, well, see Numbers, chapter16. It is a story of massive genocide at the hand of Jehovah; two hundred and fifty men burned alive, their entire families and possessions as well as those who sided with them, buried alive, swallowed up by the earth, and a plague that killed nearly fifteen thousand. All because they dared to approach Jehovah with their concerns. Mass murder was as easy for Jehovah as the wave of a finger.

PERIOD OF THE JUDGES: 1496-1016 BC

Period Number Two:
480 Years From the exodus to King Solomon's
fourth year to reign

"And it came to pass in the four hundred and eightieth year after the children of Israel were come out of the land of Egypt, in the fourth year of Solomon's reign over Israel, in the month Zif, which is the second month, that he began to build the house of the Lord." (I Kings 6:1)

This period of four hundred and eighty years began with the exodus from Egypt. The first forty years were spent in the wilderness led by Moses. The last eighty-four years saw the first kings who ruled: King Saul's forty years, King David's forty years, and King Solomon's first four years. During the years between the exodus and the kings, the judges or priests were in control.

Some of the more familiar judges were Joshua, Deborah, Gideon, Samson, Eli, and Samuel. Per Jehovah's instructions, Samuel, the last judge to rule, anointed the first king in Israel, King Saul.

The judges, or priests, were descended from Jacob's third son, Levi. Moses and his brother Aaron were Levites. Not all Levites were priests, but all priests were Levites. The priests had the responsibility of offering sacrifices to Jehovah and performing other rites and rituals as well as conferring with Moses and Aaron on civil matters that required a judgment be made. Moses remained the intermediary between the judges and Jehovah.

There is a plethora of historical and very interesting information contained within the Old Testament books relating to the period of the judges both during and after Moses's death: stories of battles for land, manna from Heaven, water from rocks, Aaron's golden calf, infighting and disputes, and doubts in and disobediences to Jehovah replete with the harshest of punishments. One of the most notable events is Moses's foray into Mount Sinai where Jehovah gave him the ten commandments etched on stone tablets. The stone tablets bearing the ten commandments were housed in a sacred, well-guarded object which in turn was housed in a sacred, well-guarded structure. Both were constructed by the order of Jehovah and built to his precise specifications. The object enjoys worldwide fame. It was the Ark of the Covenant. The structure housing the Ark was the Tabernacle.

The Ark of the Covenant was a box the size of a small casket made of acacia wood and overlaid with gold both inside and out. Two winged cherubs faced each other atop the ark. I envision the cherubs as representing the positive and negative posts that functioned like the plus and minus posts on a car battery. At any rate, as one ham radio operator put it, from the structure and components described in the Bible, the Ark of the Covenant could easily have been a shortwave radio/receiver. There are points which support this probability.

In the first place, it was strictly forbidden for anyone to touch the Ark. To do so meant death. Could that have been due to high voltage? Years later, during the reign of King David when the Ark was being moved on a cart, the oxen stumbled, and the Ark was in danger of falling to the ground. A man named Uzzah reached out to prevent its fall, and as soon as he touched the Ark, he died. Could it have been due to electrocution? Additionally, Jehovah verbally communicated with Moses through or from the Ark. See Exodus 25:22 and Numbers 7:89. The sound of Jehovah's voice came from the Ark.

At each corner of the Ark were rings for inserting poles on both sides so that the priests could carry it. When the Israelites were on the move, the priests carried the Ark before them. The Ark went before the Israelite army when it went into battle. When the Ark went before them, they won the battle. When the Ark did not go before them, they lost. When the Israelites were not on the move, the Ark sat at rest within the Tabernacle.

The Tabernacle was a temporary, portable structure. Whenever the Israelites moved camp, it was dismantled and moved with them. This occurred forty times during their forty years in the wilderness. It seems that the Tabernacle was somewhat of a parking garage for Jehovah whenever he descended from his position within the cloud above the encampment.

The Tabernacle was a tent facing an open courtyard containing the sacrificial altar. There were two sections within the tent. One area was where the priests performed required rituals and sacrifices. The rear section was where the Ark was kept. Priests were allowed in that area only once a year. The entire compound was surrounded by a fence of elaborate fabrics stretched between posts overlaid with gold and other metals. Most of the artifacts, the candlestick or menorah, the table, an altar, etc., were overlaid in gold or other precious metals. There were very strict rules concerning when and when not to approach the Tabernacle. When Jehovah was present, his cloud surrounded the tent. Only Moses could approach. No cloud meant that Jehovah was not present.

Aside from occasionally housing Jehovah and housing the Ark of the Covenant and other religious artifacts, the Tabernacle served as the seat for offering sacrifices and gifts and prayers or praises to Jehovah. Many different replicas of both the Ark and the Tabernacle have been created and are currently on display around the world.

PERIOD OF THE KINGS: 1016-586 BC

Period Number Three: 430 Years
From King Solomon to the fall of Jerusalem to Babylon

The terms saga, odyssey, epic tale, etc. do not begin to describe the era of the kings in Israel, and there were many of them within this four hundred plus year period. Most of the kings were evil, maniacal and put heavy burdens on their subjects. They began to pull away from Jehovah and to worship multiple gods. The masses began to lose faith in Jehovah, and moral decadence began to corrode the once powerful nation. Sound familiar?

Jehovah chose Saul to be the first king, and Samuel appointed him. Saul was from the tribe of Benjamin, Jacob's youngest son. Saul's first action, in keeping with Jehovah's demand, was that of war. "Now go and smite Amalek and utterly destroy all that they have, and spare them not; but slay both man and woman, infant and suckling, ox and sheep, camel and ass." and Saul "took Agag the king of the Amalekites alive, and utterly destroyed all the people with the edge of the sword."

Saul proved to be a very evil king. He did not remain obedient to Jehovah so that both Jehovah and Samuel regretted having made him king. Eventually, Saul was wounded in battle and his three sons killed. Saul killed himself by falling on his sword.

Israel's second king was David of the tribe of Judah. It was David who could calm King Saul's violent moods by playing for him on the harp. It was also David, the shepherd boy, who famously slew the Philistine giant, Goliath, with a stone from his slingshot. David was Jehovah's 'golden boy.' David was loyal to Jehovah. David wrote many of the Psalms found in the Old Testament. And it was from David's lineage that Jesus was born more than six hundred years later.

David's son, Solomon, known for his wisdom, was Israel's third king. One well-known story is recorded in I Kings 3:16-28. Two women brought an infant before Solomon for a judgment, each claiming to be the mother of the child. Solomon asked for his sword, saying he would cut the child in half and give each woman half of the child. Solomon knew which was the real mother when the real mother withdrew her claim, and he gave that woman the child.

As had been prophesized, Solomon began the construction of a new temple in Jerusalem in his fourth year to reign. This event signaled the ending of one era and the beginning of another, the ruling of the kings, "the iniquity of Israel" which, as Jehovah pointed out to Ezekiel, lasted for a period of four hundred and thirty years. (See Ezekiel 4:3-7)

Solomon lived a very lavish lifestyle; to do so, he heavily taxed his subjects. He turned away from Jehovah and began to worship other gods. In fact, pagan idolatry and immorality began to be widespread in Israel. Faithlessness in Jehovah, Biblical illiteracy, rebellion, lack of spiritual discernment--the nation of Israel was in a state of decay. Again, does this sound familiar?

When Solomon's son, Rehoboam, became king, the people thought things would improve. Instead, things became worse. Civil war erupted. The ten northern territories or tribes broke away from or seceded from the statehood of Israel and became the Northern Kingdom or the House of Israel. Their first king was Jeroboam. The two remaining tribes, the tribe of Benjamin and the tribe of Judah, became known as the Southern Kingdom or the House of Judah. In the north, the Levites or priests were rejected in favor of idol worship. The Levites gave up all their land and possessions in the northern territories and moved into the southern kingdom. From that point on, each House had it own succession of kings.

The Northern Kingdom or House of Israel was eventually overthrown by Assyria, and the Israelites were literally deported and sent into what is today, Syria. These are the fabled or supposed lost tribes of Israel. The House of Israel and its fall has no bearing on the timeline being presented here so will not be discussed.

Our timeline follows and ends with the fall of the House of Judah. The king in power at the time was Zedekiah. The invading nation was Babylon. Babylon's king at the time was the well-known Nebuchadnezzar II. The date was 586 BC.

Charts at the back of the book give complete references for the recorded events that this author used to calculate the Bible's timeline. I have presented both forward and reverse timelines on the following two pages. A more simple summary is at the back.

THE BIBLE'S
REVERSE TIMELINE

The starting date and the dates of Nebuchadnezzar II are taken from recorded historical records as reported in Collier's Encyclopedia and many other sources.

586 BC: Nebuchadnezzar II, King of Babylon from 605-561 BC, in his nineteenth year to reign, overran Jerusalem and captured King Zedekiah, king of the House of Judah in his eleventh year to reign. Zedekiah was the last king to rule in Israel. II Kings 24

430 years earlier...

1016 BC: This date marked the beginning of the idolatrous kings. Jehovah referred to it as the "iniquity of Israel" and it lasted four hundred and thirty years. This period began in the fourth year of King Solomon's reign when he began to rebuild the temple in Jerusalem. Ezekiel 4:3-7

480 years earlier...

There were four hundred and eighty years between Solomon's fourth year to reign and the exodus.

1496 BC: Year of the exodus from Egypt....I Kings 6:1

430 years earlier...

The Israelites were in Egypt for four hundred and thirty years.... Exodus 12:40

1926 BC: Israel entered Egypt. Jacob was one hundred and thirty years if age....Genesis 47:28

2056 BC: Jacob was born 2108 years after Adam. (Genesis 5-47, see chart at back)

2108 years earlier...

4164 BC: Adam appeared....Genesis 2:7

THE BIBLE'S
FORWARD TIMELINE

4164 BC: Adam appeared on Earth. He was the first of a hybrid race of *homo sapiens* initiated and maintained by the entity Jehovah. This race became known as the Israelites. Various terms have been loosely attached to certain of Adam's descendants such as Hebrews, Semites, and Jews. The era of the patriarchs lasted for 2108 years as recorded in the book of Genesis.

(See complete references at the back of the book.)

2108 years later...

2056 BC: The patriarch Jacob was born. Jehovah later changed Jacob's name to Israel. His descendants became known as the Israelites.

1926 BC: At the age of one hundred thirty years, Jacob took his sons and their families to Egypt and took up residence in the territory of Goshen.

430 years later...

The Israelites were in Egypt four hundred and thirty years. (Exodus 12:40)

1496 BC: The Exodus. The Israelites exited Egypt led by Moses and Aaron

480 years later...

1016 BC: Four hundred and eighty years after the exodus, the building of the temple in Jerusalem began in King Solomon's fourth year to reign. (I Kings 6:1-2)

430 years later...

586 BC: King Nebuchadnezzar II, in his nineteenth year as King of Babylon, routed Jerusalem, destroyed the temple, and captured Zedekiah, the last king in Israel, in his eleventh year as King over the House of Judah, the southern kingdom of Israel. (II Kings 24 and 25)

PART THREE

THE REVEAL

Before going further, I want to reaffirm my personal religious/ spiritual philosophy in order to get you on track with me, so to speak. This is not to influence you in any way, rather, to clarify for you what influences me. This is the third book I have written expressing my ideas about God and man. All contain much the same information but each from its own perspective and each with its own emphasis. I suppose that my rationale is that eventually, someone will read and either agree with or at least appreciate my admittedly anti-traditional philosophy. Bear in mind that I do not believe that anyone else must believe as I do. I am not interested in influencing anyone's beliefs or in validating my own by convincing others to see things my way. But maybe, just maybe, someone who is searching will find my suggestions palatable, even welcomed.

Since I do claim to be a protestant Christian, I must accept that my beliefs are certainly untraditional. However, that is not to say that my ideas are to be scoffed at as being off the wall, worthless, frightening, or dangerous. Consider this wisdom from Judaism's Talmud: "Who is wise? One who learns from all." In my search for spiritual understanding, this is what I continue to do. I listen to all.

My concern is that many will see my ideas as being heretical, a spear in the heart of religion, specifically, Christianity. This is far from the truth. I know that certain of my loved ones pray continuously for the salvation of my soul. I thank them for their prayers on my behalf. But my soul must walk its own path toward its goal, reunion with God. And I do fervently hope that the path that my loved ones and friends are on will see them to their goal.

I believe that everything that exists, everything, began or emanated from a single source. Man can only theorize as to what that source is and how it began. We, I, refer to the source as the Creator or as God.

After all other aspects of the physical Earth were set in motion, God made man and made man in *His* own image. For this reason, we assume that mankind is God's ultimate living creation, at least here on Earth. Most of us consider God to be spiritual in nature. So, being made in the image of God, man is therefore a spiritual being as well as a physical one. Man's spiritual self, or soul as we call it, is not tangible as is his physical self. It offers no visible evidence that it exists. Yet we *know* that it does. We *know* this intuitively. And we *know* that it represents the true self.

The physical world represents a schooling or a testing for the soul. To exist within and experience the physical world, the spiritual self is housed within a physical body which allows it to relate fully to the material world. When the physical body dies, the spiritual self lives on. But where does it go? We don't really know.

Remember what we learned in junior high science? Matter can neither be created nor destroyed, it can only be changed. The physical body is matter, so when it, as we say, dies, it is not transformed into nothingness. It is simply changed in form. It goes, if I may borrow a phrase, from dust unto dust. So, even if it is destroyed, it continues in different form.

If the physical aspect of our being lives on, then it stands to reason that the even more significant aspect of ourselves, the spiritual self or soul, also continues to exist. If it has become fully enlightened, which is a rarity, it is reinstated and returns to its source, to God. That *is* the inborn goal of all souls. Through its earthly experiences, if not fully restored to its innate goodness, it's apparent if only symbolic condition at birth, then it must continue to strive toward that outcome. After completing an unsuccessful lifetime, the soul may want to return to Earth and try again or it *may* qualify for entrance into a higher realm for schooling and testing of a different, more advanced nature. It is the soul that makes this determination for itself. Individual need and karma are factors.

As I see it, through our life experiences and the way in which we build or neglect to build upon those experiences, each of us constructs our own individual gateway into eternity. Our gateway is indicative of our soul's development. Our life experiences are the building stones. They must be carefully selected and just as carefully set in place. Use of the right stones will result in a strong structure. Some stones, however, will be insufficient. Often, a selected stone will prove to be useless and must be discarded. Sometimes, the walls of our gateway simply collapse and we must begin again. No two gateways are exactly alike and everyone is responsible for building his or her own. Yes, we may accept help in the building but the completion remains the responsibility of the individual.

The floor or foundation of my gateway is God. I want to repeat that. My personal foundation is God, not Jesus, not religion, not prophecy, not fear of hell, not good deeds, not what is traditional or trending; simply, God. The capstone awaiting the completion of my gate is Heaven or wherever God is. My life experiences are the building stones. Over the years, I have gathered many stones. Some have had to be cast aside. Others have proven to be quite satisfactory in helping to form a strong and valid ideological structure.

I do, however, understand that I will probably not complete my gateway to eternity in my current lifetime. More time, lifetimes, will likely be required. Yes, be advised, completion of our gateways, our way back to God, requires numerous physical lifetimes for most of us. This is by being born again, by reincarnation.

Because it is so thoroughly misunderstood by so many, the idea of reincarnation is erroneously feared and abhorred. Reincarnation is simply a rebirth of the soul or the soul returning to the physical world by entering a newborn physical body, being born again. A soul cannot become fully enlightened until it has experienced all aspects of physical life; being male, being female, being wealthy, being poor, being ignorant, being wise, being of high character, being of criminal mind, being murdered, being a murderer, being a variety of races, etc. Jesus himself said, "A man must be born again." I believe he meant that literally as well as figuratively.

Before you get all flustered, angry, frightened, or disgusted, how many times have you said, though jokingly, "in my last life" or "in my next life"? What if this is the reality? How many times have you experienced *deja vu*, felt as though you had been in a certain situation before or that you were witnessing or doing something all over again? Subconsciously, we *know* things that we do not know we know. Psychology has its own explanation. But the soul *knows* what the reality is. For the most part, our physical minds are not aware or conscious of what the soul knows, but occasionally, we get a glimpse.

When adversity finds its way into our lives, most of us weep and wail and think, "Poor me!" or "Why is God punishing me?" But the soul knows and accepts that we are simply reaping the seeds that we sowed in a former lifetime. The soul also knows that how we conduct ourselves in our current lifetime is forming the blueprint for a future life. This prospect bears our serious attention and concern.

I have given you a brief look at my personal philosophy regarding God, soul, reincarnation, and karma. But this writing is concerned with just one of these. This writing concerns God. It is concerned not with what God is, for no one knows this. This writing is focused on what God is not.

My active search for truth began when I read that the Biblical Adam lived a mere six thousand years ago. Either this information is not true or the church's teaching about Adam being the first man is not true. I started searching the Christian Bible for the answer.

As you have seen, I did find the Bible's timeline which told me that Adam appeared a little over six thousand years ago. Armed with this knowledge, it was education coupled with my God-given sense of rationale that assured me that Adam was not the first man. He was not the father of mankind as the church touts. But it does appear that he was the first of a unique race of mankind. My mind was relieved to finally settle this issue. However, there were other questions seemingly without answers. The following questions are just a few that greatly troubled me:

How did a lump of clay become an intelligent, living organism, and what did it look like?

Why did [God] tempt Adam and Eve by placing the forbidden fruit in the Garden of Eden? Why was it placed in the very center of the garden?

Did Adam and his immediate descendants really live for hundreds of years? Why does this seem to concern no one other than myself?

What does it mean that Enoch did not die but was "taken" by God?

Excluding Noah and his family, why did [God] decide to destroy all life, even the animals by flooding the [whole] Earth?

How could forty days of rain destroy the entire Earth? And there were many other questions, as I have previously noted, concerning Noah and the story of the flood.

Why would [God] require the sacrifice of living things including humans, in particular, Abraham's only son?

How could a man, Jonah, remain in the stomach of a whale for three days without being digested?

Why did [God] harden the heart of the pharaoh if [He] really wanted [His] children freed from bondage and out of Egypt?

After the loyalty Moses had shown him, why did [God] deny Moses entry into the Promised Land and command him to die though Moses's physical strength and vitality had not ceased? How *did* Moses die?

Why did [God] boast that He was "a manly god of war" and a "vengeful god?" Why did [God] punish severely even to the point of mass murder?

There are so many, many seemingly *unanswerable* questions. But there is one explanation that answers them all. Before you say: "We cannot understand God's ways"; "It's a mystery"; or "We simply must have faith in Him," let me say that faith in God does not include blindly accepting the atrocities perpetrated by the Old Testament entity, Jehovah. I have faith that God is the Creator of the all. I have faith that the essence that is God is all-forgiving, all-loving, non-violent, omniscient, omnipotent, and omnipresent.

The actions and characteristics attributable to the god of the Old Testament go against everything I have been taught about God. You see, I *know* that God does not experience anger, remorse, or regret. I *know* that God does not seek revenge or retribution. I *know* that God does not seek praise and adoration. I *know* that God does not promote war. I *know* that God does not punish, murder or maim. I *know* that God does not require the sacrifice of living things; He is the giver of life, not a taker. Neither does God favor some of mankind over the rest. All are made like Him by Him.

In my search to discover Adam's date of appearance, I made an even more crucial discovery that has put my mind to rest about the many un-godlike characteristics and actions of [God] as [He] is presented in the Old Testament of the Christian/Judean bibles. All my questions and doubts were resolved with this reveal: The god of the Old Testament is not, cannot be, God our Creator. The god of the Bible is not, cannot be, God our Creator. Jehovah was/is *not* God our Creator. My soul had been telling me this all my life. Finally understanding this, my heart is no longer heavy.

I believe that I have presented a timeline that clearly demonstrates that if the Bible is a true historical record, then Adam came into being around six thousand years ago. And since Adam came into being a mere six thousand years ago, he cannot have been the first man on Earth. Adam was the first of a new race of mankind, but he was not the beginning of mankind. Additionally, I have presented plausible explanations for my arguments against various traditional, ludicrous interpretations of certain events. Discussing various troublesome issues was the focus of the first book of this writing. But the most significant question was and is, "Is the god of the Old Testament of the Bible God our Creator?" If not, then aren't Christianity and Judaism worshipping a false god?

I believe that I have adequately defended the reality that the evil-minded god of the Old Testament of the Bible, Jehovah, is not the instrument that brought the all into being, is not the essence we refer to as God. The god of the Old Testament was/is a physical entity. God our Creator is a spiritual essence. With this understanding, the troublesome questions have all been answered. God was not the author of the Biblical story. God was not the "vengeful man of war" about which the Old Testament revolves.

My explicit purpose for writing this and other of my books is to offer a little clarity regarding God and man, the Bible and religion, salvation and eternal life to anyone caught in a spiritual dilemma as to what they can or should believe. I have attempted to eliminate the myth and mysticism by entertaining plausible explanations in order to establish a possible/probable reality. Personal belief remains just that, personal. Each of us must discover our own path to spiritual understanding.

Three questions remain: Is the Bible the Word of God? Was Jesus God? Is there only one path to eternal life?

Note: I did tell you that I would offer my theory of how Jonah could have survived three days in the belly of a whale. The answer came to me after watching movies like, "The Hunt for Red October," "Gray Lady Down," "The Enemy Below," and "Run Silent, Run Deep." I was struck by the resemblance of the sight of a submarine surfacing, to the sight of a whale surfacing. Then, when I learned that one can exit a submarine while it remains deeply submerged, swim around, and reenter the submarine I understood the story of Jonah in the whale. Jonah had to have been taken into a sub-marine vehicle of some kind and let out three days later. Having never seen a sub-marine vessel, and knowing nothing about motorized vehicles, Jonah described his experience as having been swallowed by a whale. End of mystery!

BOOK TWO

PART ONE

IS THE BIBLE
THE WORD OF GOD?

I have literally heard, so it is not hearsay, the interview of a world-renown evangelist in which he declared that he believes every word in the Bible is true and is the Word, verbatim, of God. That astounded me. I have said that I believe all the events recorded in the Bible, though inaccurately interpreted in many cases, took place. And I certainly believe that all the numerical information was diligently and accurately recorded. The Bible's timeline adds up to me. But a verbatim transcription of God speaking to hundreds of writers, translators, and transcribers over thousands of years, no. Not possible.

Well, wait a minute, because with God all things are possible. But in this case, we have got to apply our God-given common sense. Applying our common sense does not imply a lack of faith or lack of belief in God. Even faith is controlled by our sense of rationale. We cannot prove that God exists, yet our common sense tells us that He must. And this transmutes into what we refer to as having faith; accepting the unseen, the unknown, even the unknowable.

The manner in which the early Biblical narrative is presented does seem to imply a single narrator as none of the characters, other than Jehovah, speak to us in the first person. Oddly, even the supposed writer of the first five books, Moses, takes the third person approach. He doesn't use "I" or the first person when speaking of himself. He uses his name, Moses, as though someone else was doing the narrating.

Most Christians mistakenly believe that King David wrote the Psalms. Bible scholars have determined that at least eight men authored the Psalms and probably more as there are many anonymous poems. These poems, generally written in the first person, are praises to the God of Israel, Jehovah. Did Jehovah dictate these tributes to himself? It wouldn't be surprising but it is highly unlikely.

The same is true of the Proverbs. Solomon usually receives the credit, but, like the Psalms, Bible scholars know that there were multiple authors. The narration of the scriptures covers thousands of years, is recorded in various languages and has been worded and reworded by an indeterminate number of translators and transcribers. I think that we can safely assume that no single entity is responsible for the Biblical scriptures, neither the Old Testament nor the New Testament.

If it *was* God doing the telling, there would be no need for editing. Yet despite numerous warnings in the Bible about adding to or taking away from its narrative, man has edited the words of the Bible/God repeatedly and continues to do so. And these edits are not done from the original languages but strictly from man's own ideas of how to modernize the Bible. An example is the NIV, the *New International Version*. Why edit God's words? Granted, newer versions are much easier to read than, for example, the Old English of King James's translators. Hast, wast, sayest, doeth, goeth, thee, thou- these are Old English words not found in ancient languages. How do we know that *original* meaning has not been compromised?

Theologians get around the multiple author problem by saying that the words are not necessarily the *words* of God but were *inspired* by God. Yet we continue to refer to the scriptures as the Word of God as though God spoke through the various authors. Certainly, much of the scriptures was written by men inspired by their relationship with their God based on their conception of God and His role in their lives. But they wrote in their own words, not God's.

We *can* believe that the Old Testament of the Bible is a record of the history of a singular race of man, the Israelites, today's Jews. We can also assume that like the history of any nation or race, the record is slanted, told in a manner favorable to that nation or race and from the perspective of the author. But that is not to say that the record is false or faulty. Though there are minor discrepancies here and there, I do believe that the Protestant Old Testament and the Jewish Tanakh are reliable records of Adam's descendants. Inspired by God? Possibly. But narrated by God? No.

How can I so adamantly claim that the Bible is not the Word of God? Because, as I have made the point previously in this writing, the god presented in the Old Testament, who apparently had a hand in its writing, is not God, not the source of all creation. The god of the Old Testament is not even *a* god. Would the God you know and love claim to be a "manly god of war" or a "vengeful god?" The god of the Old Testament is an imposter claiming to be God Almighty (his own words to Moses). The god of the Old Testament is an entity of unknown origin but apparently not of this earth. He has given us his name, Jehovah. He wishes to be known as Jehovah until time indefinite.

Jehovah came to Earth from somewhere in space and, observing humans, decided to do his own experimenting. He was probably attempting to produce a subservient group of earthly beings who would serve him here on Earth according to his every demand. But the human gene would not conform and his plans were thwarted. He has since left the Earth. Whether he will return is not known but that is a possibility.

By his lack of compassion and his lack of the ability to love, by the very cruelty and evil that was his nature, it is obvious that Jehovah was/is not God, not the God of our creation. So, even if Jehovah did narrate either all or some of the contents of the Old Testament, the contents do not represent the words of *God*.

In researching the life of Jesus, I noted various errors and inconsistencies that I consider to be very strong verification that the Bible is *not* the Word of God, but the words of ordinary men recounting their experiences and even third parties retelling other men's experiences and stories. This is certainly true of the New Testament, the Christian message. There are too many inconsistencies between and among the various authors' accounts for the accounting to have come directly from God. Man was at work here.

One example is an account recorded in both Matthew and Mark, KJV, of an incident with Jesus and his disciples. In Mark 8:27-29: "And Jesus went out, and his disciples, into the towns of Caesarea Philippi: and by the way he asked his disciples, saying unto them, Whom do men say that I am? And they answered, John the Baptist: but some *say*, Elias; and others, One of the prophets. And he saith unto them, But whom say ye that I am? And Peter answereth and saith unto him, Thou art the Christ. And he charged them that they should tell no man of him."

Referencing the same event, in Matthew 16:13-17: "When Jesus came into the coasts of Caesarea Philippi, he asked his disciples, saying, Whom do men say that I, the Son of man am? And they said, Some *say that thou art* John the Baptist: some, Elias; and others, Jeremias, or one of the prophets. He saith unto them, But whom say ye that I am? And Simon Peter answered and said, Thou art the Christ, the Son of the living God. And Jesus answered and said unto him, Blessed art thou, Simon Barjona: for *flesh* and blood hath not revealed *it* unto thee, but my Father which is in heaven."

Two accountings of the same incident each with its own phrasing and emphasis yet each version is to be considered the words of God, the Word of God? It is acceptable for two men to tell a story in different words. But would they also quote God differently? Am I making too much this? I don't think so. I am merely stressing the point that the scriptures were written by men, not dictated to man by God. The scriptures represent experiences of men as told in their own words or the words of another. And yes, many of them were inspired by their belief in God. Then of course, much editing of the original writings has been done by different thinkers who think differently. The Bible is certainly an inspired writing, but it is written not in the words of God but in the words of men.

The Bible is not a holy book written by the finger of God. The Bible is a history book with the New Testament being a well-deserved memorial to the man, Jesus, to his life and teachings as told neither in his own words nor in the words of God but in the words of others, many others.

But the fact that the Bible continues to exist despite the many efforts over time to destroy it and its message is certainly by the grace and the will of God. Nevertheless, it is by the words of men that the Bible was written. And it is in the words of men that it continues to be rewritten to this day.

PART TWO

WAS/IS JESUS GOD?

There is not a lot that we know about Jesus. But before we get into who Jesus was I wish to point out what most Christians do not realize about the most authoritative record of his birth and life, the New Testament of the Protestant Bible. The New Testament is not a continuation of the scriptures of the Old Testament. It is not a modern translation of ancient scriptures written in ancient languages.

Judaism emerged from Old Testament scripture which it considered to be the word of God. And although there are instances in the New Testament which seem to fulfill Old Testament prophecies, the New Testament is not based on scripture. The New Testament scriptures came *after* the beginning of the Christian movement, which was directly attributable to the *followers* of Jesus. Except for the writings of Paul, portions of the New Testament were written by various latecomers to the Christian movement and continued to evolve as the movement grew. We can see the necessity of Christianity attaching its writings to the Jewish scriptures to give their own writings the illusion of being the continuing [Word of God].

The New Testament is a modern-day construct written primarily by Saint Paul, a Jew, and by various anonymous writers. It is thought that the four gospels, Matthew, Mark, Luke, and John, were written not by the apostles or disciples whose names they bear but by various unknown, unnamed authors much later than the times and events they portray. And I have read that the Old Testament portion of the Christian Bible, though based on the Jewish Tanakh, is a retooling of the Jewish scriptures to make them compatible with the New Testament narrative. But what is of the utmost importance is the fact that Jesus did not write, or even dictate, any of it. He left no written documents or spoken instructions, period.

There are many mentions of Jesus in non-biblical writings. Both Jewish and Roman records of the time acknowledge that the Biblical man Jesus, a Jew and a teacher, did exist though the circumstances of his birth and life as depicted in the New Testament are disputed. But the New Testament is the only Biblical record of the man Jesus of which I am aware. So, what does it tell us about Jesus?

The first book of the New Testament, Matthew, begins with the genealogy of Jesus, tracing his heritage back to the patriarch Abraham, up through King David to Joseph, husband of Mary the mother of Jesus. It continues with the story of the virgin Mary conceiving and the birth of Jesus in the Judean town of Bethlehem just south of Jerusalem.

In the third gospel, Luke, in the third chapter we are given the genealogy of Jesus through his supposed father, Joseph, back through King David, through Abraham, and summarily, all the way back to Adam, the son of [god].

It is very interesting *and* alarming that the two genealogies do not agree with one another. From King David forward to Jesus, at least nine patriarchal generations, they do not agree in a single instance. This is because one genealogy follows King David's son, Solomon, and the other follows King David's son, Nathan. In Luke's account, the well-known King Solomon is not mentioned at all.

I have read that one of the genealogies is that of Mary, the mother of Jesus. I don't know how or by whom this was suggested. But, unless one of them *is* Mary's, then we do not have a record of Jesus' lineage. Think about it. Even if one of the two genealogies working up to **Joseph** *is* correct, then we still do not have a record of Jesus's lineage, since Joseph, according to scripture, was not the father of Jesus. So if we want to connect Jesus back to the early House of David, one of these two records must be Mary's. Oddly, she is not mentioned in either. Of course, women were not considered when tracing one's lineage. But in this case, you would think that there would have been an exception. At any rate, we are left to decide for ourselves which, if either record is to be considered.

The fact of the matter is that Jesus's ancestry does not matter at all. Neither do the circumstances of his birth, or his death. They have no bearing on who the man was and what resulted from his existence. His historical importance cannot be doubted.

But to the Jews of his time, his lineage was very important. There are numerous passages in the Old Testament/Tanakh scriptures which supposedly prophesy the coming of a savior. Jews anticipated a king who would lead the nation of Israel to power, and he would come from the lineage of King David of the House of Judah.

When Jesus began his ministry, it became apparent that he was not a king. The controlling Jewish establishment of the time rejected Jesus. And today's Jewish establishment continues to reject him as the one prophesized in the scriptures who would save Israel.

At the time of Jesus's birth, there were no Christians. At the time of his death, there were no Christians. I want to repeat that, "At he time of Jesus's birth and of his death, there were no Christians." In the geographical area around which the Biblical narrative of Jesus is centered, there were Jews and Gentiles. Gentile simply meant a non-Jew, an outsider, a non-believer, a heathen, a Pagan. Judaism was based on the belief that there is but one God. Other religions popular at the time supported the belief in multiple gods.

Another point of interest is that at the time, the belief in the existence of angels and demons and many lesser gods, as well as the idea of transmutation among these entities, was prevalent and accepted. Angels could be transformed into humans and humans into angels, even *gods*. What we equate to being folk tales and myths were taken very literally and seriously. The idea of reincarnation, too, was readily accepted. We have verification of this in Matthew 16:13-17 and in Mark 8:27-30. It was believed by his followers that Jesus was the reincarnation of one of the former Jewish prophets.

Remember, Christianity came about *after* the crucifixion of Jesus. As the followers of Jesus grew larger and larger in number, his *philosophy* became a movement unto itself and was eventually given the name Christianity. Keep in mind that it was not Jesus himself who started this *new religion.*

Basically, the movement was *begun* by Jesus's disciple, the apostle Peter. It was expanded by various disciples, primarily Paul, and other followers. Interestingly, it was the Greeks who contributed greatly to Christianity's expansion. The Greek Orthodox Church is touted by many to be the oldest Christian religion. At one time, the Christian Bible was written totally in Greek. Incidentally, it was the Greeks who coined the word, Hell.

So, Christianity was initiated by Jews. Eventually, the man Paul, also a Jew and later dubbed Saint Paul and thought of as a Gentile, abandoned the Jewish teachings and became the primary contributor to the spread of early Christianity. But it is important to remember, Jesus did not leave behind any instructions or writings on which to base a new religion. And most of his teachings were in the form of metaphors, analogies, and symbolic figures of speech. His words were certainly open to interpretation.

This new religion, and Christianity *is* a new religion, has been shaped and formulated over the years since its inception by numerous bodies of men, each believing that their own interpretation of the Biblical Jesus and his message is not only the correct interpretation but the only acceptable interpretation.

Thankfully, what has become standard Christian theology adheres basically to the message that Jesus brought to the world, and that is that God is the reality, one God, and that He is the God of the whole of mankind. And that by accepting this reality, one is assured eternal life.

Christianity knows that there is but one God. However, does Christianity believe that God is the God of all, or that He is the God of Christians only? Is the Christian God the father of Muslims? Is the Christian God the father of Buddhists? Is the Christian God the father of Jews who do not accept Jesus as Christianity sees him? That is the question we have got to consider. And until we can say and believe, "Yes, God is the father of *all* men," we, as Christians, cannot move forward spiritually.

How does Christianity see God? Christianity teaches that God is a three-in-one entity; the Father, the Son, and the Holy Ghost. It does not separate the three. The Trinity-this is a concept older than written history that was the basis for innumerable early religions most of which were very un-godlike and heathen in their practices.

How does Christianity see Jesus? It appears that Christianity claims that Jesus was God come to Earth. And many Christians have relegated God to the background as they pray *to* Jesus, ask for *his* blessings, and thank *him* for the blessings they receive.

It appears that Christianity believes that Jesus is God, based on the very first verse of chapter one of the Gospel of John, KJV: "In the beginning was the Word, and the Word was with God, and the Word was God." The "Word" is thought to refer to Jesus, therefore, Jesus is God, or at least an aspect of God. This verse has been interpreted as meaning that God is a trinity of personalities embodied within a single entity.

You will recall earlier in this writing my reference to *The New World Translation of the Holy Scriptures*, the Bible used by Jehovah's Witnesses. I have stated that, for the most part, both this version and the King James Version agree, though there are minor differences here and there. But minor differences can undermine major differences. For example, the above-quoted verse as it reads in the NWT: "In [the] beginning the Word was, and the Word was with God, and the Word was *a god.*" Wow! What a difference a tiny word and a lowercase letter make! Both versions were translated from the original languages. In translating the KJV, however, earlier interpretations were considered. The NWT was translated directly from the original languages with no consideration of other translations or interpretations. But who is to say which, if either version, or any version represents truth, or reality?

So, whatever the basis, combined with the ideology of the Trinity, Christianity believes that Jesus was God come to Earth in the form of man. Funny, but I was taught that God has never come onto the earth and certainly not in physical form. I cannot reconcile these two claims with one another. Can you? Again, it is just "One of those mysteries man is not capable of understanding." I believe that such statements as, *"it is a mystery"* or *"man cannot understand"* or *"it is not meant for man to understand,"* are mere excuses that translate into shortcomings of Christian thinking. Christianity must pay attention to details and consider their meaning. Christianity must not lean on its own understanding as long as that understanding is clouded in mystery. God is not a mystery. He has made truth available to man. Jesus came to Earth to bring the truth concerning the reality of God and His relationship to man. This was apparently his reason for being born. The titles Savior and Christ were given to Jesus by his followers. And Jesus lived up to these deserved titles of respect even unto death, even after death.

I believe that Jesus was an enlightened soul, subordinate only to God. From the very beginning, he sat at the right hand of God. The spiritual realm was the only existence his soul had experienced. God, as a help to mankind sent this most beloved son/soul to Earth. This enlightened spiritual being, this soul, took on a physical body so that he could understand the material world and man's role in it. He was to witness to the truth that God does exist, to witness that every man is a child (son or daughter) of God, and to assure mankind that eternal life is the reality for all who, through faith, accept this. While in Heaven, this enlightened soul did not look like the man Jesus and was not called by the name Jesus. On coming to Earth and entering into the newly born infant that was given the name Jesus, God's favorite son became as all men, a flesh and blood being subject to the rules of the material world.

I continue to believe that the essence that is God, although all around us and within us, has never come to earth as an entity in physical form. So, was/is Jesus God the Creator? For the answer to this question, I yield to Jesus's own words. For ease of understanding, I have taken the following quotes from the NIV, the *New International Version* of the Bible:

"The living Father has sent me, and I live because of the Father."
John 6:57

"I came from God and now am here. I have not come of my own accord, he sent me." John 8:42

"I came from heaven, not to do my own will, but to do the will of him that sent me." John 6:38

"For as the Father has life in himself; so he has given the Son life in himself and has given him the authority to judge man because he is the Son of man." John 5:26-27

"For the Father does not judge man but has given judgment to the Son of man." John 5:22

"My teaching is not mine, but it is his that sent me." John 7:16

Jesus replied, "These words you hear are not my own; they belong to the Father who sent me." John 14: 24

"I am the vine and my Father is the garden keeper." John 15:1

"For the Father loves the son and shows him what He does." John 5:20

"No man has seen the Father, only he which is sent from God, has seen the Father." John 6:46

"All things have been committed to me by my Father." Matthew 11:27

"Even though they have seen my works they have hated both me and my Father." John 15:24

The woman said, I know that Christ is coming. Then Jesus declared, "I am he." John 4:25,26

(Jesus prayed) "<u>My Father</u>, if it is possible may this cup be taken from me. Yet not as <u>I</u> will, but as <u>you</u> will." Matthew 26:39

"<u>I came from the Father</u> and entered the world; now I am leaving the world and <u>going back to the Father</u>." John 16:28

"<u>I go to the Father</u> because <u>my Father is greater than I</u>." John 14:28

"And now, Father, <u>glorify me in your presence</u> with the glory <u>I had with you</u> before the world began." John 17:5

. . . and the high priest asked him, **"Are you the Christ?" "I am,"** said Jesus. **"And you will see the <u>Son of Man</u> sitting at the right hand of the Mighty One."** Mark 14:61-63

If Jesus *was* God come to Earth, Jesus *is* God. Did Jesus create man?
Is Jesus God?

Note: On March 28, 2018, I had a heart attack. I was rushed to a cardiac center where I was promptly taken in for a heart catheterization. I was not nervous or afraid. In fact, I was very glad for the prompt response and procedure. As I was moved onto the operating table my attention was drawn to a bright area on the ceiling. As I looked up I saw an oval-shaped area the size of a football that was brightly lit with soft yellow-white light. At the center was God in profile. He was sitting on a large stone, not on a throne. He was bearded, robed, and was looking straight ahead, to my left, as if looking into the distance. At His right side, and a bit lower, sat Jesus. Jesus was leaning toward God and looking up into His face. Both were solid gold. Was this an epiphany or was it induced by my frame of mind and the conditions at the time? The reader may decide. As for me, it was solid vindication that my belief in God as a singular entity and the sole creator is the reality and that, my love for

Jesus notwithstanding, my adoration of God and God alone as the creator of the all is a righteous belief.

PART THREE

IS THERE ONLY ONE PATH TO ETERNAL LIFE?

Though I have read different versions of it, to me one of the most profound statements ever made concerning one's religious beliefs is that made by Mohandas Karamchand "Mahatma" Gandhi. When asked if he was a Hindu, he replied, "Yes, I am, and I am a Muslim, a Christian, a Buddhist, a Taoist, and a Jew." Wow! Regarding God's relationship to man, that says it all. All people are God's people.

When it comes to religion, the desire for world domination seems to be the goal. It's a harsh indictment, but nevertheless, it does seem to be the goal of the world's three major religions, Islam, Judaism, and Christianity.

Christianity hopes and strives for world domination. Judaism expects and waits for world domination. Islam demands world domination, death to all infidels-it is written-smite them at their necks.

The truth is one's religious beliefs and practices, other than influencing one's lifestyle, have no bearing on the goal of attaining everlasting life. But one's spirituality does. Gandhi knew this. He also understood that there are many pathways toward spiritual enlightenment. I agree with Gandhi. He said, **"What does it matter that we take different roads so long as we reach the same goal?"** And what is the goal? To spend eternity with God rather than sink into oblivion or some other undesirable state.

Does the Christian New Testament say anything about how to attain everlasting life? It does indeed! The book of John emphasizes that the only thing necessary for gaining everlasting life is belief, belief in the Son of God, belief in Jesus. If you believe in Jesus, you will have faith in his teachings. If you have faith in his teachings, you will have faith or belief in God. It really is that simple. But the religion of Christianity has expanded that requirement: you must be born again, you must be washed in the blood of Christ, you must repent, you must confess, you must be baptized, and on and on. I personally believe that belief is the only requirement.

It is easy to believe in Jesus. He was a flesh and blood being. History verifies the fact that he lived. It is not as easy to believe in our unseen God. It requires faith on our part. How do we establish in our minds and hearts the kind of faith *devoid of fear* (many are afraid *not* to believe in God/Jesus) that it takes to believe in the unseen, the unknown, the unknowable? There are many ways, many roads as Gandhi said, to spiritual growth and understanding.

I like to keep in mind these words of Jesus in John 14:2: "In my Father's house are many mansions: if it were not so, I would have told you. I go to prepare a place for you." In other words, in Heaven, not only is there room for all, a place has been prepared for all.

Different religions, as well as life itself, provide different pathways to spiritual understanding and growth *or* lack thereof. Spiritual discernment is the key, and each man and woman must follow his or her own heart, listen to his or her own soul, walk his or her own path, travel his or her own road.

Note: Obvious, to me, Mahatma Gandhi was an old soul, as we say, and as such was far advanced up the ladder toward spiritual understanding. I must take seriously his words regarding Christianity. As a Christian myself, I find the following words especially painful. Gandhi said: "I like your Christ. I do not like your Christians. Your Christians are so unlike your Christ." But I believe this observation can be made within all religions. We all need to strive more diligently toward spiritual understanding. The world is in great need of it.

THE BIBLE'S CHRONOLOGY

Adam's Appearance
(2238 years later)

Jacob/Israel at 130 years of age enters Egypt.
(430 years later)

The Exodus: Israel exits Egypt.
(480 years later)

The period of the judges ends.
The period of the kings begins.
(430 years later)

King Nebuchadnezzar, II captures King Zedekiah
586 BC
(430 years earlier)

King Solomon begins building the temple in Jerusalem.
1016 BC
(480 years earlier)

The Exodus
1496 BC
(430 years earlier)

Israel enters Egypt)
1926 BC
(2238 years earlier)

Adam appears in Eden.
4164 BC

	BORN				DIED		
	Age At Son's Birth	Years After Adam	Years Before Christ	Total Age	Years After Adam	Years Before Christ	Reference: Book Of Genesis
ADAM	130	--	--	4164	930	930	3234	5:3-5
SETH	105	130	4034	912	1042	3122	5:6-8
ENOS	90	235	3929	905	1140	3024	5:9-11
CAINAN	70	325	3839	910	1235	2929	5:12-14
MAHALALEEL	65	395	3769	895	1290	2874	5:15-17
JARED	162	460	3704	962	1422	2742	5:18-20
ENOCH	65	622	3542	365	987	3177	5:21-24
METHUSELAH	187	687	3477	969	1656	2508	5:25-27
LAMECH	182	874	3290	777	1651	2513	5:28-31
NOAH	502	1056	3108	950	2006	2158	7:6, 11 9:28-29
SHEM	100	1558	2606	600	2158	2006	11:10-11
NOAH AT FLOOD	600	1656	2508				7:6, 11
SHEM AT FLOOD	98	1656	2508	FLOOD OCCURED			11:10
ARPHAXAD	35	1658	2506	438	2096	2068	11:12-13
SALAH	30	1693	2471	433	2126	2038	11:14-15
EBER	34	1723	2441	464	2187	1977	11:16-17
PELEG	30	1757	2407	239	1996	2168	11:18-19
REU	32	1787	2377	239	2026	2138	11:20-21
SERUG	30	1819	2345	230	2049	2115	11:22-23
NAHOR	29	1849	2315	148	1997	2167	11:24-25
TERAH	70	1878	2286	205	2083	2081	11:26 11:32
ABRAHAM	100	1948	2216	175	2123	2041	21:5 25:7
ISAAC	60	2048	2116	180	2228	1936	25:26 35:28-29
JACOB	--	2108	2056	147	2255	1909	47:28

JACOB'S NAME CHANGED TO ISRAEL. 35:10

ISRAEL ENTERS EGYPT AT AGE 130. . . . . 47:28

*This reference states that Enoch was taken by God unlike his kinsmen who simply died. The inference is that Enoch did not experience physical death rather, ascended unto his god.

PERIOD OF THE KINGS

The Iniquity of Israel

The House of Judah

In Ezekiel 4:4-7 it is recorded that the iniquity of the house of Israel lasted for 390 years. The iniquity of the house of Judah lasted for the same 390 years plus 40 years longer for a period of 430 years.

THE KINGS	NUMBER OF YEARS RULED	REFERENCE
Saul	40	Acts 13:21
David	40	II Sam 5:4/I Kings 2:10
Solomon	3.5 (480 years of judges ends)	I Kings 6:1-2
Solomon (430 Year Rule of Kings Begin)	36.5	I Kings 11:42
Rehoboam	17	I Kings 14:21
Abijah (Abijam)	3	I Kings 15:1-2
Asa	41	I Kings 15:8-10
Jehoshaphat	25	I Kings 15:24 / 22:41-42
Jehoram(Joram)	8	II Kings 8:16-17
Ahaziah	1	II Kings 8:25
Athalia (Motherof Ahaziah)	6	II Kings 11
Jehoash (Joash)	40	II Kings 11:21-12:1
Amaziah	29	II Kings 14:1-2
Azariah (Uzziah/Uzza)	52	II Kings 15:1-2
Jotham	16	II Kings 5:32-33
Ahaz	16	II Kings 16:1-2
Hezekiah	29	II Kings 18:1-2
Manasseh	55	II Kings 20:21-21:1
Amon	2	II Kings 21:18-19
Josiah	31	II Kings 21:24-22:1
Jehoahaz (Jeconiah)	25	II Kings 23:30-31
Jehoiakim (Eliakim)	11	II Kings 23:34, 36
Jehoiachin	25	II Kings 24: 6, 8
Zedekian (Mattaniah)	11	II Kings 24:17-18
TOTALS	430	**Ezekiel 4:4-7**

In King Solomon's fourth year to reign, he began rebuilding the temple in Jerusalem. This was the beginning of the next period of the Bible's time table. Israel was divided into the two kingdoms, Israel and Judah, during Solomon's son, Rehoboam's, rule. In Zedekiah's eleventh year to reign, Nebuchadnezzar of Babylon, in his nineteenth year to reign, after two years of besieging Jerusalem, overtook the city, destroyed the temple that Solomon had built, captured, and imprisoned King Zedekiah in Babylon. *This occurred in the year 586 BC.*

That God which ever lives and loves,
One God, one law, one element,
And one far-off divine event
To which the whole creation moves.

Author Unknown

CPSIA information can be obtained
at www.ICGtesting.com
Printed in the USA
FSHW01n0527030518
47517FS

9 781681 112367